THE BATTLE OF GETTYSBURG

150 Things to Know

0 11557 01281 1

The Battle of Gettysburg

150 Things to Know

Sandy Allison, editor

STACKPOLE
BOOKS

Published by
STACKPOLE BOOKS
5067 Ritter Road
Mechanicsburg, PA 17055
www.stackpolebooks.com

Printed in the United States of America

10 9 8 7 6 5 4 3 2 1

First edition

Cover design by Tessa J. Sweigert
Cover photo © Shutterstock

Library of Congress Cataloging-in-Publication Data

The Battle of Gettysburg : 150 things to know / Sandy Allison, editor. — First edition.
    pages cm
  ISBN 978-0-8117-1281-1 (pbk.)
1. Gettysburg, Battle of, Gettysburg, Pa., 1863—Anecdotes. 2. Gettysburg, Battle of, Gettysburg, Pa., 1863—Miscellanea. I. Allison, Sandy.
  E475.53.B3453 2013
  973.7'349—dc23
                                    2013013743

CONTENTS

Lee Moves North

Invading the North Was a Sound Idea

In the spring of 1863, the future of the Confederacy looked grim. Union armies controlled vital Southern ports—New Orleans, Memphis, and Norfolk—and Vicksburg was under siege. After more than two years of fighting, the South's resources were rapidly depleted, and its railroads couldn't move what supplies were available to where they were needed most. The commander of the Army of Northern Virginia, Robert E. Lee, was having trouble providing his troops with food, clothes, weapons, and ammunition.

Even so, Lee's army had recently scored dramatic victories at Fredericksburg and Chancellorsville, leaving Union troops demoralized and their leadership in disarray. It seemed like the perfect time for a bold move—an invasion of the North. Such a campaign would draw the Federal Army of the Potomac away from Richmond; it might even threaten Washington, a storehouse of supplies, and force the Union to move troops away from Vicksburg, weakening their siege. It would disrupt transportation and communication systems and throw fear into the civilian population, perhaps causing them to clamor for peace. Most importantly, it would allow the Confederate army to take advantage of the rich farmlands of Maryland and Pennsylvania; as they moved, the Southern soldiers could live off the land.

By mid-June, vast numbers of Confederate infantrymen were marching into Maryland near Williamsport. The northern invasion was under way.

Harrisburg Was a Key Target

On June 21, Confederate general Richard Ewell received orders "to take Harrisburg." The city, the capital of Pennsylvania, is situated on the eastern bank of the Susquehanna River, which runs from north to south above the city, northwest to southeast below. It was a key transportation center. The Pennsylvania Railroad was one of the major lines linking New York and Philadelphia with western states by way of Harrisburg and Pittsburgh. Harrisburg was also a key junction for the Philadelphia and Reading Railroad; the Cumberland Valley Railroad; and the Harrisburg, Portsmouth, Mount Joy, and Lancaster Railroad.

Darius Couch, newly appointed commander of the Union's Department of the Susquehanna, worked to prepare the city's defenses. On June 15, he requested supplies and tents for ten thousand men, ten thousand rifles with full equipment, and two million rounds of ammunition. He also asked permission to call on the public to meet the emergency without regard to time of service.

Couch knew the broad Susquehanna was the invaders' major obstacle. He considered the area south of the river, from the west bank to the Maryland line, as lost. He hoped that his frantic preparations in Harrisburg would prevent the Confederates from crossing the river and reaching the rest of the state, as well as those to the north.

York's Safety Came at a Price

A Confederate brigade under John Gordon entered York, Pennsylvania, on the morning of June 28, a Sunday. "The church bells were ringing," the general remembered, "and the streets were filled with well-dressed people. The appearance of these church-going men, women, and children in their Sunday attire strangely contrasted with my marching soldiers. Begrimed as we were from head to foot . . . it was no wonder that many of York's inhabitants were terror-stricken." Gordon's commander, Jubal Early, rode into York later that day. Under orders to requisition supplies, Early told city leaders that York's safety would come at a price. A civilian remembered that the general "made a levy upon the citizens, promising, in the event of its being complied with promptly, to spare all private property in the city; otherwise, he would allow his men to take such things as they needed, and would not be responsible for the conduct of his men while they remained in the city.

"The beef, flour, and other articles, and $28,000 in money were speedily collected and handed over to the rebels. The general expressed himself satisfied with what he had received and scrupulously kept his word."

Stuart Left Lee in the Dark

Lee had intended that his cavalry under J. E. B. Stuart march along the west side of the Blue Ridge Mountains, screening the movement of the Confederate infantry and keeping him informed about the disposition of Union troops. But the discretionary orders Stuart received were interpreted by him to permit an adventuring jaunt around the Federal army, which he had done several times before. As a result, he was out of touch with Lee, didn't know where the main Federal columns were, and couldn't get promptly to Lee the information he did have. Throughout most of the northern invasion, Lee was in the dark concerning his enemy's exact whereabouts and movements.

A Burning Bridge Spoiled Invasion Goals

On June 28, John Gordon decided to cross the Susquehanna River using the Wrightsville Bridge, some twenty-five miles below Harrisburg. "My immediate object was to move rapidly . . . to the river," he wrote, "then along its right bank to the bridge, seize it, and cross to the Columbia side. Once across, I intended to mount my men, if practicable, so as to pass rapidly through Lancaster in the direction of Philadelphia." Jubal Early also planned to use the bridge "to cross the Susquehanna, levy a contribution on the rich town of Lancaster, cut the Central Railroad, and then move up in rear of Harrisburg."

Both men's plans were spoiled. On June 27, the bridge had been rigged with explosives as part of the plan to defend Lancaster County. When Gordon attacked Union soldiers near Wrightsville, they retreated rapidly across the river. As the last of the men passed the arch where the explosives were placed, the fuses were lit. Although the first explosion did little damage to the structure, barrels of kerosene were rolled out and ignited, and the bridge was quickly engulfed in flames. Gordon's column was halfway across before the conflagration drove them back. Without sufficient firefighting equipment, they couldn't prevent the bridge's destruction. The near shore of the Susquehanna River was as far north as the Confederate army would advance.

Startling News Changed Lee's Plans

By June 28, six Confederate divisions were in the area of Chambersburg, fifteen miles north of the Pennsylvania-Maryland border, and Lee himself was situated just east of town. He still intended to concentrate at or near Harrisburg. That evening, however, he received some startling news: the Union army was near Frederick, Maryland, on the east side of the mountains, and was coming his way instead of staying put in Virginia, as Lee assumed they would. He also learned that the Army of the Potomac was now under the command of George Meade, who replaced Joseph Hooker, whom Lee had defeated decisively two months before at Chancellorsville. Lee knew Meade was a savvy leader not prone to reckless mistakes.

The Army of Northern Virginia was scattered within a rough triangle between Chambersburg, Harrisburg, and York. Unless they could be quickly concentrated, they could quite possibly be defeated piecemeal by advancing Federal troops. New orders were sent at once to assemble in the vicinity of Cashtown, which lay near a pass through the mountains on the Chambersburg-Gettysburg turnpike.

Gettysburg Was a Thriving Hub

Gettysburg was a thriving small town in the years before two armies met there. Named after Samuel Gettys, who opened a tavern in the vicinity in 1761, it was established as the county seat in 1800, when the region that became Adams County seceded from York County. It was home to a number of manufacturing businesses, as well as banks, shops, and hotels, all surrounded by farms, orchards, and forested hills. In 1860, it had a population of some 2,400. It was also a hub for travel: ten different roads led into the town—an important reason why a great battle was fought there.

The South Approached from the North

As the Army of Northern Virginia marched through Maryland and Pennsylvania, the Army of the Potomac maneuvered to stay between it and Washington to prevent any move against the capital. When the fighting began at Gettysburg and both armies raced to the scene, the Confederates streamed down from the north and the Union came up from the south.

Enemies Spotted Each Other on June 30

The first meeting between Union and Confederate troops at Gettysburg was on June 30, the day before the main battle began. On that day, Confederate general James Pettigrew was ordered to take his brigade from Cashtown into Gettysburg, some ten miles to the southeast, to look for supplies, especially shoes. On his approach, Pettigrew discovered a Union cavalry force, and the sound of drums in the distance alerted him to the possibility of enemy infantry nearby. Under the circumstances, Pettigrew did not enter the town. He returned to Cashtown and reported to his superior, Henry Heth, who decided to take his entire division to Gettysburg the next day to secure the shoes he believed were there. Confederate general Ambrose P. Hill approved the mission, and Heth's troops set out at five the next morning.

But Pettigrew's actions on June 30 had alerted Meade to the Confederate threat. The cavalry Pettigrew spotted in Gettysburg were two of Union general John Buford's brigades that had arrived in town just before the Confederates approached. Buford quickly reported the enemy activity to his superiors, who were encamped farther south.

Bad Shoes Were a Common Complaint

Shoes were the most important item to troops on the march, and keeping armies equipped with serviceable footwear was no easy task. Even when they were available, Civil War–era shoes were often ill-fitting and stiff. They pinched the feet and caused blisters, turning every step into torture. One soldier described the agony: "Oh the horrors of marching on blistered feet! Heat, hunger, and thirst are nothing compared to this torment. When you stand, you seem to be on red hot iron plates; when you walk, you grimace with every step. . . . The best soldiers become nearly mutinous with suffering. They snarl and swear at each other; they fling themselves down in the dust, refusing to move a step further."

Veterans learned to soak new shoes in water and let them dry on their feet, forming a tighter fit. If a blister did develop, it was lanced with a needle threaded with wool to wick out the liquid.

The First Day

The Cavalry Held the High Ground

At 8 AM on July 1, Heth's men approached Herr Ridge, just northwest of Gettysburg. Waiting for them were Buford's dismounted cavalry troops and two cannons. The firing started, and the Confederates moved forward slowly, gradually pushing the cavalrymen back to McPherson's Ridge, nearer town. More and more troops came down the Chambersburg Road from Cashtown; by 9:30 AM, a total of thirty-five hundred Confederates were advancing, supported by twenty cannons. Buford's men numbered seventeen hundred.

As the Southerners gained ground, the small-arms fire increased. Buford watched from a vantage point in the cupola of the Lutheran Theological Seminary on a rise behind his line. His men were doing all they could to stop the advance, but in the west he could see great clouds of dust indicating even more Confederate troops on the way. He sent a stream of messengers south to Meade and corps commander John Reynolds requesting immediate assistance, but he had no idea when help would arrive or how long his troops could keep the Confederates out of town.

First-to-Fire Cannon Honors Buford

The very first cannon shot at Gettysburg was fired by John Calef, commanding Battery A of the 2nd U.S. Artillery, which was attached to Buford's cavalry division. Calef fired his 3-inch Ordnance Rifle No. 233 along the Chambersburg Pike on July 1. The tubes of this cannon and three others that fired early that day were placed around the base of the monument to Buford dedicated on July 1, 1895. Calef, a West Point graduate who won a brevet promotion for his actions at Gettysburg, participated in the dedication ceremony.

The Battle Began in an Unusual Way

Unlike most Civil War battles, Gettysburg was a "meeting" engagement; neither army was concentrated in a defensive position, and the battle developed as troops rushed to the scene along a series of roads that led to the town from Chambersburg, Carlisle, Harrisburg, and York in Pennsylvania; and Hagerstown, Baltimore, Taneytown, and Emmitsburg in Maryland.

Union Infantry Arrived Just in Time

At about 9:45 AM, Buford spotted Reynolds galloping ahead of the Army of the Potomac's 1st Corps. Upon reaching the seminary, Reynolds, one of the Union's most able and best-loved generals, consulted with his relieved cavalry commander, made a quick survey of the field, and decided that this high ground was as good a spot as any to meet Lee's army. He sent his own message to Meade: "I will fight them inch by inch, and if driven into town I will barricade the streets and hold them as long as possible."

A Shortcut Sped Up Reinforcements

After meeting with Buford, Reynolds went off to direct the arrival of reinforcements. Galloping back the way he came, through town and out again to the south, he ordered the men with him and any others he could lay hands on to proceed through the fields diagonally to the northwest, tearing big gaps in all the fences there, making a shortcut for the arriving infantry—otherwise, these troops would have to go straight north, through the cramped streets of the town, then at right angles back out to the west. Fast as they arrived, desperately needed troops bypassed the town and headed through the fields toward the sound of the guns.

Buford's Vantage Point Still Stands

The most famous building on the battlefield, the Lutheran Theological Seminary's Schmucker Hall was used by both armies throughout the battle. It was from the hall's cupola, the highest structure in the area, that Buford watched the Confederates' initial advance down the Chambersburg Pike and greeted Reynolds. The building was built in 1832. It served as a hospital during the fighting, and both Federals and Confederates were treated there. The hall and its famous cupola still stand, as part of the still-operating seminary. Tours of the cupola are offered twice a year, but space is limited, and the cost is more than a hundred dollars per person.

Buford Received a Deathbed Promotion

John Buford participated in a number of battles before Gettysburg, but it was in Pennsylvania that he had his finest hour. He is widely seen as one of the Union's heroes, credited with quickly identifying the key positions and leading his men to protect them. After Gettysburg, Buford led engagements against Lee across Virginia, but in November 1863 he contacted typhoid fever and his health rapidly declined. In December, Lincoln made him a major general just before he died.

A Regiment Was the Standard Fighting Unit

A regiment of soldiers was the practical fighting unit in both armies during the Civil War. At full strength, a regiment generally comprised about one thousand men. Each regiment was numbered and named for the state in which it was mustered (the 7th Virginia, the 14th Connecticut, and so on). Four to six regiments made up a brigade, which included around five thousand men. Three to five brigades were organized into a division, which were organized into corps. During the Battle of Gettysburg, the Army of Northern Virginia comprised three infantry corps, with three divisions in each. The Army of the Potomac was made up of seven somewhat smaller infantry corps, with three divisions in each. Both armies included cavalry corps as well as organizations of artillery attached to the various infantry groups.

The Union Quickly Lost One of Its Best

As soon as the 1st Corps arrived on the battlefield, its men were positioned along McPherson's Ridge. When the 2nd Wisconsin regiment, part of the storied "Iron Brigade," reached the crest, it was hit by a tremendous volley from Confederates led by James Archer who were running up the western slope, which at that spot was thickly wooded. Seeing his men waver, Reynolds dashed up to order the troops forward. "For God's sake," he yelled, "get those fellows out of those woods!" The 2nd Wisconsin attacked and briefly halted the Confederate advance. Reynolds turned to see if reinforcements were coming from the east—as he did he was shot in the neck and killed instantly.

Additional troops did soon arrive, and they eventually turned the flank of Archer's line and took a number of Southerners, including Archer himself, prisoner. A monument to John Reynolds now stands just east of what was renamed Reynolds Woods.

Reynolds Had Offered Meade Full Support

A veteran of the Mexican War, Reynolds was one of the most respected generals in the Union. When the Civil War started, he was commandant of cadets at West Point, in charge of both northern and southern commanders-in-training, a situation that became impossible as the fighting intensified. A native Pennsylvanian, he was given command of a brigade and acquitted himself well but was taken prisoner at Gaines' Mill. Held for several months, he was released in a prisoner exchange, perhaps because the mayor of

Fredericksburg, Virginia, petitioned for his parole—Reynolds had briefly served there as military governor.

At the Battle of Fredericksburg, in December 1862, Reynolds led a valiant charge against a strong Rebel line but was eventually turned back. In May 1863, the general traveled to Washington, where he met with Lincoln about the Army of the Potomac's leadership. Historians believe the president offered Reynolds command of the entire army at the meeting and that he turned it down. When Reynolds heard that Lincoln had installed Meade as commander, he put on his dress uniform and went to Meade's headquarters to pay his respects. Reynolds' pledge of full support gave Meade comfort in the days leading up to Gettysburg.

The Iron Brigade Changed the Fighting

When the Iron Brigade arrived on the field, the tenor of the fighting seemed to change. Until then, the Rebels faced only dismounted cavalry, and many were under the impression that their path through the town and beyond would be relatively unimpeded. The troops led by Solomon Meredith were battle-hardened infantrymen, however, with a reputation as fierce fighters. Unlike other units, the Iron Brigade wore distinctive black, broad-brimmed hats. When Archer's attacking Confederates saw this headgear, they realized they were in for a fight. One was heard to remark, "Hell, that ain't no milishy—that's the Army of the Potomac!"

A Curious Teenager Learned of Reynolds' Death

The landscape south of Gettysburg features rolling fields punctuated by high ridges. One of the most effective ways for the Union army to communicate with leaders in Washington was by using flag-waving signal corps stationed on prominent overlooks. These signalmen were posted near Emmitsburg and Frederick, Maryland, and their coded "reports" could be seen from a great distance. Civilians could see the signals too, of course, and when sixteen-year-old Emmitsburg resident George Humerick went to investigate signaling near his home on July 1, he was the first civilian to learn that Reynolds had been killed during the intensifying struggle across the Pennsylvania border. (His curiosity didn't end there—after the battle, Humerick hiked to the battlefield and managed to shake Meade's hand.)

An Elderly Civilian Joined the Fighting

Union soldier Thomas Chamberlain had first-hand knowledge of how Gettysburg civilian John Burns became part of the first day's fighting. "Our attention was called to a man of rather bony frame . . . who approached from the direction of town moving with a deliberate step and carrying in his right hand an Enfield rifle." The man, Chamberlain remembered, looked to be about seventy years old and was wearing "dark trousers and waistcoat, a blue swallow-tail coat with burnished brass buttons such as used to be affected by well-to-do gentlemen of the old school . . . and a high black silk hat."

Burns was eager to join the fighting, Chamberlain said. When asked by a general if he could shoot, the man answered, "If you knew that you had before you a soldier of the War of 1812 who fought at Lundy's Lane you would not ask such a question."

The man was sent into the woods to join the Iron Brigade. "In answer to the question what possessed him to come out there at such a time, he replied that the rebels had either driven away or milked his cows, and that he was going to be even with them," another soldier recalled. "Burns got behind a tree and surprised us all . . . He was as calm and collected as any veteran."

A Railroad Cut Became a Trap

While the Iron Brigade was battling Archer's men on the Union left, the Union right was threatened by a brigade led by Joseph Davis that made a series of successful charges against troops from Pennsylvania and New York. The right of Davis' line was stopped only when three Union regiments positioned to the south wheeled and attacked to the north. Suddenly exposed to musket fire in their flank, two Southern regiments made a terrible mistake. They jumped into an unfinished railroad cut, thinking it would offer protection. But it served only to corral the men—once they got in, they discovered that the sides were too steep for them to get out. For the Union troops, had they attacked, it would have been like shooting fish in a barrel. Instead, they called on the Confederates to surrender. It was an easy choice for many and so they laid down their arms. In total, about 225 men were taken as well as 7 officers from Davis' brigade.

A House and Its Tenants Were Caught in the Crossfire

At the southern edge of the battlefield was a colonial mansion known as the Old McLean Place. In it lived Amelia Harmon and her aunt; they had decided to stay put when the shooting began. At first, the area around the house was controlled by Confederates, who didn't enter the building. But later in the morning, Harmon remembered, "a sudden violent commotion and uproar made us fly in quick haste to the lower floor. There was a tumultuous pounding of fists and guns on the kitchen door, and loud yells of 'Open, or we'll break down the door!'

"We drew the bolt, and in poured a stream of maddened, powder-blackened bluecoats who ordered us to the cellar while they dispersed to various west windows throughout the house. From our cellar prison we could hear the tumult above, the constant crack of rifles, the hurried orders, and, outside, the mingled roar of heavy musketry, galloping horses, yelling troops, and the occasional boom of cannon."

After many anxious moments, the two heard a "swish like the mowing of grass on the front lawn, then a dense shadow darkened the low, grated cellar windows. It was the sound and shadow of hundreds of marching feet. We could see them to the knees only, but the uniforms are the Confederate gray!" Harmon and her aunt rushed from the house unharmed, eventually making their way to safety in the rear of the Union line. But the house and its barn were set ablaze and destroyed.

Hospitals Were Set Up Almost Immediately

Even as the fighting raged, the wounded were taken to hospitals hastily set up in homes and other buildings. One resident remembered the scene upon emerging from her cellar after hearing soldiers enter the upstairs rooms bearing injured comrades. "In many cases carpets were so saturated with blood as to be unfit for further use. Walls were bloodstained, as well as books that were used for pillows."

She also noted that "the first public building that was opened for hospital purposes was the Lutheran Church on Chambersburg Street, generally known as College Church. Forty men were laid in the lecture room and 100 in the church proper, beds being improvised by laying boards on top of pews."

Confederate Gray Wasn't Standardized

At the time of the Battle of Gettysburg, the usual Confederate army uniform consisted of a gray jacket or frock coat and light blue or gray kersey wool trousers. There were no summer uniform pants of lighter material. As the war progressed, supplies were hard to come by, and Confederate soldiers often wore civilian "make-do" clothing and captured Union accoutrements. The Confederate gray color was not standardized; it varied widely, ranging from light to dark, sometimes with a brownish or bluish tint.

Union army uniforms were more standardized. A four-button sack coat was common, but a dress frock coat was often issued, too. Coats were dark blue. Kersey wool trousers were usually light blue, sometimes dark blue.

Soldiers Sported Distinctive Headgear

The iconic flat-topped caps worn by infantrymen in the Civil War are similar to two types of older military headgear. Most Union soldiers in the East wore "forage caps," which derived from the tall stovepipe "shakos" worn by U.S. soldiers in earlier conflicts. Forage caps were generally shapeless and had either straight or curved brims. Confederates, as well as a good number of Federals, wore a "kepi," which was trimmer and had less material than a forage cap. They were derived from the stiff, round hats worn by French soldiers throughout the nineteenth century.

The Advantage Shifted to the South

As the fighting along McPherson's Ridge continued, superior Confederate numbers and well-executed maneuvers began to turn the battle's tide. Conditions seemed to change around half past two, according to Thomas Chamberlain, "when the rebel batteries began to increase the rapidity of their fire. A glance to the west showed the troops of Heth's and Pender's divisions in motion, descending rapidly . . . regiment upon regiment *en echelon*—followed by supporting columns extending as far as the eye could reach. Their advance was magnificent, and as mere spectators or military critics we might have enjoyed or applauded it, but it boded evil to our scanty force.

"The enemy drew nearer and nearer, firing rapidly as he came, but was met by a resistance which time and again staggered him, though it could not shake him off."

Pickets and Skirmish Lines Were Valuable

Warfare tactics at the time of the Civil War made wide use of pickets and skirmish lines. In general, any large group of troops always had a scattered line of soldiers surrounding it—these pickets were deployed well away from the main body of troops, but close enough so that easy communication between the pickets and the main unit was possible. Pickets were the first to detect enemy movement near a body of troops; they served as advance guards to warn of danger. This hazardous duty was usually rotated among individuals in a unit.

Similarly, when a large group of soldiers moved forward, a loose line of skirmishers usually went first to probe enemy defenses and draw enemy fire. In theory, skirmishers were to be deployed as groups of four soldiers, each standing five feet apart, with about forty paces between each group of four; but in reality, terrain and other circumstances usually determined the configuration.

The importance of skirmishers is illustrated by Alfred Iverson's ill-fated charge on July 1. The Confederate general sent his brigade on the attack without deploying skirmishers, and the unit was mowed down when hidden Federals opened fire; some nine hundred Rebels were lost in the charge. A line of skirmishers would almost surely have discovered the unseen soldiers and prevented the brigade from marching into the ambush.

Barlow Failed to Defend a Small Knoll

As Confederate infantry began arriving from the north and northeast of town, the fighting shifted in that direction. Ordered to shore up defenses on the right of the Union line, division commander Francis Barlow decided that the best place to position his men was on a small hill near the Harrisburg Pike. His decision proved disastrous, however, as it created a bulge in the Union line that could be attacked from two sides. That's exactly what happened: George Doles' brigade hit Barlow from the left, and Gordon's brigade attacked from the right. Barlow's troops were routed, and the general was wounded and captured in the melee. When the Federals retreated in disarray, the entire Union line weakened, eventually falling back bit by bit in defeat. Barlow's decision was greatly criticized after the battle, and it's unlikely to ever be forgotten—the patch of high ground he struggled to defend was renamed Barlow's Knoll.

An Acquaintance Was Made in the Midst of Battle

John Gordon told of a poignant battlefield encounter as his men fought Union troops north of town. "In the midst of the wild disorder in his ranks, and through a storm of bullets, a Union officer was seeking to rally his men for a final stand. He, too, went down, pierced by a Minie ball. Riding forward with my rapidly advancing lines, I discovered the brave officer lying upon his back with the July sun pouring its rays upon his pale face. He was surrounded by Union dead, and his own life seemed to be rapidly ebbing out.

"Quickly dismounting and lifting his head, I gave him water from my canteen, asking him his name and the character of his wounds. He was Major General Francis C. Barlow, of New York. . . . Neither of us had the remotest thought that he would survive many hours. I summoned several soldiers who were looking after the wounded and directed them to place him upon a litter and carry him to the shade in the rear."

Unknown to Gordon, Barlow survived his wounds. A year after the battle, Barlow learned that a J. B. Gordon had been killed near Richmond. Although this was a relative of the Gordon he had met in Gettysburg, Barlow assumed it was the same man. A dozen years after the war, Barlow met Gordon in Washington, and Gordon inquired, "Are you related to the Barlow who was killed at Gettysburg?" Barlow answered, "I am the man, sir. Are you related to the Gordon who killed me?" Said Gordon: "I am the man, sir!" The two became good friends.

The Union Made a Confused Retreat

As the attack on Union forces north of town built to hurricane force, one of the mounted Confederate reserves waiting behind the line described the action: "Soon the rebel yell could be distinguished in the mighty roar, and conveyed to us the gratifying intelligence that our boys were getting the best of the fight; and a signal officer of a station nearby soon verified the fact that the enemy was retreating from every position.

"Then the welcome order came for us to quickly advance to the front . . . and we spurred our horses along the road for Gettysburg. Through the timber, across a small stream—and the battlefield was before us in all its horrors and excitement.

"In our front were open fields and orchards, and a little further on, the town. Many pieces of artillery occupied the high ground to our right, but their thunder was silenced now, while the heaps of dead and dying . . . told how the boys in blue had bravely stood by their guns. A little beyond, to judge from the windrows of the dead, a Union regiment had been blotted out. Along the road the blue and gray veterans lay thickly. . . . Dashing forward, we came up with our infantry, driving Howard's corps through the town. Confusion seemed to reign in the Federal ranks."

The Confederates' Arrival Caused Panic

A Gettysburg resident who was fifteen at the time of the battle remembered when Confederate troops entered the town. "We were having our regular literary exercises on Friday afternoon when the cry reached our ears. Rushing to the door and standing on the front portico, we beheld in the direction of the Theological Seminary a dark, dense mass moving toward town. Our teacher at once said, 'Children, run home as quickly as you can.' It did not require repeating. . . .

"I scarcely reached the front door when, on looking up the street, I saw some of the men on horseback. I scrambled in, slammed the door shut, and, hastening to the sitting room, peeped out between the shutters. What a horrible sight! There they were . . . riding wildly pell-mell down the hill toward our home, shouting, yelling most unearthily, cursing, brandishing their revolvers and firing right and left. I was fully persuaded that the rebels had actually come at last. What they would do with us was a fearful question to my young mind."

Advancing Confederates Met Little Resistance

Confederate cavalryman Harry Gilmour remembered the weak resistance his men faced as they pressed forward. "Near the edge of town was a regiment, apparently in a very disorganized condition but still holding on to their colors. In we dashed among them, slashing right and left. Most of them gave up, or, rather, threw down their arms and continued on. A small squad of ten or more rallied around their colors. We dashed at them. Two fired upon us, but so wildly that neither horse nor man was struck. They presented their bayonets, but, after knocking these aside and cutting down two or three of them, the rest surrendered."

Stonewall Might Have Made a Difference

Lee followed his troops on July 1, eventually stopping on Seminary Ridge to survey the field. He saw apparently disorganized Union troops disappearing to the east over the crest of a ridge a mile from where he stood. He also saw that Richard Ewell's 2nd Corps had forced the Federals back through town from the north. He thought that an immediate follow-up attack by Ewell would push the wavering Union army completely off the high ground of Cemetery Hill, which was immediately south of Gettysburg.

But when Ewell received the somewhat ambiguous order to "attack that hill, if practicable," he paused along the Harrisburg Road just north of Cemetery Hill, suffering from the heat, fatigue, and pain from the infected stump of the leg he had lost a year earlier. Accustomed to serving under Thomas "Stonewall" Jackson, who gave short, unequivocal commands, but who had been killed at Chancellorsville, he was unsure how to handle the discretionary orders Lee often issued. Ewell also had it fixed in his mind that Lee wanted to avoid bringing on a full-scale engagement that day. As he hesitated, several subordinates urged him to press his attack—like Lee, they could see the tactical advantage of capturing Cemetery Hill and adjacent Culp's Hill. But he ignored their advice, deciding to stop short of the heights and wait for more troops to arrive. By the time that happened, darkness was fast approaching, and a renewed attack was postponed.

A Quick Attack on Culp's Hill Might Have Succeeded

The Confederate division led by Edward Johnson arrived in Gettysburg via the Chambersburg Pike at sunset, after a hard twenty-five-mile march. They were immediately ordered to take Culp's Hill if reconnaissance showed that it was unoccupied. Johnson sent scouts to investigate, and at about the same time, the Union division led by James Wadsworth, which had been guarding supplies behind the lines, arrived on Culp's from the opposite direction.

Wadsworth's men captured a few scouts and fired on the rest. Those not captured returned to Johnson and reported that the high ground was indeed occupied by Federals—but the strength of the enemy was not known. Johnson decided not to risk an evening battle until he could better size up the situation. Had an assault been made, historians believe that Johnson's men could well have taken the heights and significantly altered the course of the next day's fighting.

The Final Outcome Was Left in Doubt

Even though the Confederates controlled the town after the first day's fighting and had forced the Union to retreat, the final outcome of the battle was left in doubt. On the rocky heights just south of town, newly arriving Federal commanders gradually restored order to the beaten troops, and reinforcements started to bring Union manpower numbers in line with those of the Confederates. One Gettysburg civilian described the situation succinctly: "While the rebels were halting, resting, and rejoicing, the 1st and 11th Corps of the Army of the Potomac fell back upon Cemetery and Culp's Hills, undisturbed in obtaining . . . these strong natural positions."

Troops Camped among the Tombs

On the night of July 1, Union general Abner Doubleday and part of his command found themselves encamped in Cemetery Hill's namesake town cemetery, near the distinctive arched gateway that still stands today. Next to the gate was posted a sign: All Persons Found Using Firearms In These Grounds Will Be Prosecuted With The Utmost Rigor Of The Law. "We lay on our arms that night among the tombs," the general remembered, "so suggestive of the shortness of life and the nothingness of fame; but the men were little disposed to moralize on themes like these, and were much too exhausted to think of anything but much-needed rest."

Lee and Longstreet Disagreed on Tactics

James Longstreet was commander of the Confederate 1st Corps and one of the most respected generals in the Army of Northern Virginia. He remembered his meeting with Lee on July 1: "I found him on the summit of Seminary Ridge watching the enemy concentrate on the opposite hill. He pointed out their position to me. I took my glasses and made as careful a survey as I could from that point. After five or ten minutes I turned to General Lee and said, 'If we could have chosen a point to meet our plans of operation I do not think we could have found a better one than that upon which they are now concentrating.'

"'All we have to do is throw our army around by their left, and we shall interpose between the Federal Army and Washington. We can get a strong position and wait. . . . The Federals will be sure to attack us. When they attack we shall beat them . . . and the probabilities are that the fruits of our success will be great.'

"'No,' said General Lee, 'the enemy is there, and I am going to attack him there.'"

Two Confederate Corps Were Led by Inexperienced Commanders

Before the Gettysburg campaign, Lee had reorganized his two army corps into three, of which only one, the 1st, led by Longstreet, was under the control of an experienced corps commander. The other two commanders, Ewell and A. P. Hill, newly promoted from command of divisions, both showed promise based on experience but were untried in the employment of larger bodies of troops.

Longstreet concurred in the choice of Ewell for one of the corps on the basis of his rank, ability, and service. But Longstreet thought that Daniel H. Hill, of North Carolina, was A. P. Hill's superior in rank, skill, and judgment and should have been appointed corps commander instead. Next in rank was Lafayette McLaws, one of Longstreet's own division commanders and his second choice. McLaws had a distinguished battle record, but he was not in the best of health. Nor was he a Virginian, and Longstreet implied that this was a strong influence against Lee's selection of D. H. Hill or McLaws. In failing to select either, Lee had impaired the morale of his troops, Longstreet believed.

Granting Lee's right to make his own selection, the probability exists that cooperation between the Confederate corps commanders at Gettysburg would have been more effective if Longstreet's recommendations had been accepted. Indeed, historians of the battle have disclosed evidence of a lack of harmony and team spirit between Longstreet, Ewell, and Hill.

Doubleday Led Troops—But Didn't Invent Baseball

When Reynolds was killed, Abner Doubleday took over command of the 1st Corps, leading the Union defense of the town. He relinquished command to John Newton on July 2. By most accounts, Doubleday performed admirably at Gettysburg and is now remembered as an effective Civil War general. He didn't invent baseball, however. The origin of this persistent myth is a 1905 "study" of the sport organized by Albert Spalding, a sports gear manufacturer. Doubleday's friend Abraham Mills wrote much of the study's findings, which credited Doubleday with codifying the rules of the game in Cooperstown, New York, in 1839. Doubleday himself never mentioned baseball, however, and in 1839 he was at West Point—no evidence exists that he ever had leave. He couldn't object to the study, though; he died in 1893.

The Second Day

Meade Arrived on the Second Day

The commander of the Army of the Potomac reached Gettysburg very early in the morning of July 2. According to Union general Carl Schurz: "General Meade quietly appeared in the cemetery on horseback, accompanied by a staff officer and an orderly. His long, bearded, haggard face, shaded by a black military felt hat, the rim of which was turned down, looked careworn and tired, as if he had not slept that night. The spectacles on his nose gave him a somewhat magisterial look. There was nothing in his appearance or bearing—not a smile nor a sympathetic word addressed to those around him—that might have made the hearts of the soldiers warm up to him.

"There was nothing of a pose, nothing stagy about him. His mind was evidently absorbed by a hard problem. But this simple, cold, serious soldier, with his businesslike air did inspire confidence."

After Meade examined the position of the army, Schurz wrote, he "nodded, seemingly with approval. After the usual salutation I asked him how many men he had on the ground. . . . 'In the course of the day I expect to have about 95,000—enough, I guess, for this business.'"

The Union Had Seven Top Generals

When Meade reached Gettysburg, he was the seventh Union battlefield commander responsible for all the forces currently engaged there. When the firing first started, Buford was in charge until Reynolds arrived a few hours later. When Reynolds went down, Abner Doubleday assumed command. He was succeeded by 11th Corps commander Oliver Howard. Winfield Scott Hancock, commander of the 2nd Corps, was sent by Meade to take over from Howard; he arrived around half past four on July 1. His time at the top lasted until 12th Corps commander Henry Slocum came. Slocum relinquished control with the arrival of Meade.

Famous Horses Were on the Field

An estimated 30,000 horses were part of the battle—most generals were mounted, as was the cavalry, of course, and horses (and mules) were important working animals for both armies. Two of the Civil War's most famous mounts were present at Gettysburg: Lee rode his faithful Traveller, from which he famously watched Pickett's Charge; Meade rode Old Baldy, named for its white face. Both horses survived the war and were part of their masters' funeral processions. Traveller died in 1871, a year after Lee died. Old Baldy outlived Meade by almost a decade, despite being wounded in battle on four separate occasions.

Sedgwick's Corps Rushed to the Field

The largest corps in the Federal army, some eighteen thousand strong, was thirty miles away from Gettysburg when the fighting began. The men of the 6th Corps were camped in Manchester, Maryland, along the road to Baltimore, enjoying a rare day of rest. Darkness had fallen when corps commander John Sedgwick received the alarming news that a battle against the Army of Northern Virginia had begun in earnest and that John Reynolds was dead.

In the message, Meade asked Sedgwick when his men could be on the battlefield ready to fight. Sedgwick knew that under normal circumstances it would take two days for his huge force to reach the scene. But he sensed that these were not normal circumstances, so he promised his commander he would reach Gettysburg by four o'clock the next day.

The corps was assembled and sent off immediately, but heavy wagon traffic on the Westminster Road prevented it from moving much more than six miles by early morning. Sedgwick kept his men moving through the jam, and when the road was at last clear, he ordered them to march at double-quick time in the hot July sun without stopping for food or rest. At two o'clock, Sedgwick met Meade on the field; the 6th Corps followed soon after, causing cheers to break out up and down the Union line. The Federals could now face their enemy with enough troops to withstand the coming assault.

Tension Between Officers and Foot Soldiers Was Evident

A wartime resident of the Weikert house, in the midst of the battleground, remembered a telling incident about camaraderie among foot soldiers: "While the infantry were passing, I noticed a poor, worn out soldier crawling along on his hands and knees. An officer yelled at him, with cursing, to get up and march. The poor fellow said he could not, whereupon the officer, raising his sword, struck him down three or four times. The officer passed on, little caring what he had done. Some of his comrades at once picked up the prostrate form and carried the unfortunate man into our house.

"He seemed quite a young man, and was suffering from sunstroke received on the forced march. As they were carrying him in, some of the men who had witnessed the act of brutality remarked, 'We will mark that officer for this.' It is a pretty well established fact that many a brutal officer fell in battle from being shot other than by the enemy."

The Setting Was Bucolic

A Union soldier posted on Cemetery Ridge vividly described the setting in which he found himself on July 2. "By ten o'clock the threatening clouds vanished and the green meadows were bathed in sunlight, with here and there the shadow of transient clouds flitting across the sunlit valley and hills. Cattle were grazing in the field below; the shrill crowing of chanticleer was heard from neighboring farmyards; tame pigeons cooed on the hillside, and birds sang among the trees.

"The crest, as far as the eye could see, glittered with burnished arms. On our right was the cemetery with its white monuments, among which shone the burnished brass pieces of artillery and the glittering bayonets of the infantry. Beyond this were seen the spires of the town. . . . Running across our front, obliquely, was the Emmitsburg Road, while farther beyond was Seminary Ridge, on which the enemy was posted. On our left, over a mile distant, rose the sugar-loaf summits of the Round Tops."

Rainy Weather Filled the Creeks

The weather in Gettysburg the week before the battle was wetter and cooler than normal. Rain fell often from June 25 through June 27, and the creeks and streams in the area were full. Confederates had trouble crossing the largest waterway, Rock Creek, which blocked their approach to Culp's Hill, because of high water. Plum Run, which flowed between Devil's Den and Little Round Top (and was to be known as "Bloody Run"), was much more than the trickle it often is today. During the fighting, the weather was clearer and warmer, reaching close to 90 degrees during Pickett's Charge. The rains came back on July 4, however, hindering Lee's retreat across the Potomac River and making the process of burying the dead all the more difficult.

Delays Plagued the Confederate Attack

On the morning of July 2, the Confederate line stretched along Seminary Ridge, to the west of and almost parallel to Cemetery Ridge, which extended south from Cemetery Hill. The far left of the Confederate line made a wide arc to the east, curving above the northern faces of Cemetery and Culp's Hills.

Ewell was on the Confederate left, facing the heights. Hill was in the center and Longstreet on the right. Lee ordered an attack up the Emmitsburg Road on the left half of the Union line. His plan called for Longstreet to gain control of the strategic south end of Cemetery Ridge while the other two corps kept the Union center and right occupied. Confederate movements did not proceed as planned. Ewell was to hold off his attack on the two hills until he heard Longstreet's guns; he did not hear the firing until 5 PM because Longstreet had encountered problems. First, he felt he needed to wait until a supporting cavalry brigade returned from a mission, which it did around noon. Then, as engineers started to guide his troops into attack position, he discovered that the route was in plain view of the enemy. A more concealed route was found, but troops weren't in position until after 4 PM. Longstreet's attack was further complicated when Union general Daniel Sickles, in violation of Meade's orders, pulled out of the Cemetery Ridge line and advanced a half mile forward, onto what Sickles believed was better ground.

Sickles Had an Independent Streak

Daniel Sickles, the only one of Meade's corps commanders who was not a professional soldier, had formerly been a congressman from New York. He did not always think along well-charted military lines as did his colleagues who had been trained at West Point. He was a rugged individualist, infamous in some quarters for shooting and killing Philip Barton Key, the son of Francis Scott Key, author of

"The Star-Spangled Banner" (Key had allegedly toyed with the affections and honor of Sickles' wife).

There is good reason to believe that Sickles lacked Meade's confidence, which was understandable in view of the miserable showing almost universally made in their military roles by the ambitious politicians whom Abraham Lincoln was persuaded to clothe with the stars and authority of general officers.

On that background must be viewed the unilateral action Sickles took on the early afternoon of July 2, when he weakened Meade's plan of passive defense along Cemetery Ridge by moving his men forward. As a result, he unhinged the Union line on the left, exposing the vital anchor of the Round Tops to enemy capture and creating a wide gap between his troops and those on his right. When the fighting began, Sickles' 3rd Corps found itself lined up close to the enemy, parallel to but one-half to three-quarters of a mile west of the main Union line, with both flanks exposed.

Fear Was a Constant Companion

Soldiers reacted to the stress of waiting for battle in many ways. Some were silent, lost in thought; others joked to relieve the tension. Some found solace in food, or prayer. Some threw away cards, dice, or pornographic pictures, worried that they might be sent home with their personal effects should they be killed. Some were obviously fearful, reacting to orders automatically as if in a dream. "In such moments men grow pale and lose their nerve," a Federal captain wrote. "They are hungry but cannot eat; they are tired but cannot sit down. You speak to them, and they answer as if half asleep; they laugh, but the laugh has no joy in it."

Once they were in combat and felt a sense of control over their actions, many men were surprised by their calmness. One Union private remembered, "After the first round was fired, the fear left me and I was as cool as I ever was in my life."

But many carried their fear into battle. When the fighting began, their actions became confused, and they fired wildly without aiming. This was especially true of new recruits. In the First Battle of Bull Run, it was estimated that 8,000 bullets were fired for every man hit. After Gettysburg, nearly half of the 27,500 abandoned guns were found to have at least 2 unfired rounds rammed down the barrel. In panic, the owners had repeatedly loaded the weapons without putting on the percussion caps, never actually firing a round.

Both Rebels and Federals "Yelled" During Battle

During a battle, the combined smoke from rifles and cannons often obscured the field, and soldiers had to aim by the flash of enemy gun blasts or by sound—and the sounds of battle were unforgettable to any participant. Besides the thunder and rattle of the guns, the thumping and neighing of horses, and the tattoo of martial drums, the sounds of fighting included the men's shouts, screams, songs, and group yells. The famous rebel yell was variously described as a high-pitched "yip-yip" or "ki-yi" and was used throughout the war. The Federals yelled in unison, too—usually an excited "hurrah" or "huzzah." In either case, the sound made by the voices of hundreds of attacking troops served to strike fear in the hearts of the enemy.

The Attackers Were Hit Immediately

A Confederate infantryman told of attacking the Union left on July 2: "The men sprang forward as if at a game of ball. The air was full of sound. A long line of Federal skirmishers, protected by a stone wall, immediately opened fire. Grape and canister from the Federal battery hurtled over us . . .

"Men were falling, stricken to death. This soldier received on the left thigh a blow from a minie ball that was exceedingly painful, but for which he did not halt. The younger officers made themselves conspicuous by rushing to the front, commanding and urging the men to come on. . . .

"In the din of battle we could hear the charges of canister passing over us with the noise of partridges in flight. Immediately to the right, Taylor Darwin, orderly sergeant of Company I, stopped suddenly, quivered, and sank to the earth dead, a ball having passed through his brain."

Close Fighting Helped Rebel Artillery

Historians note that Confederate cannons at Gettysburg were inferior to their Union counterparts, that there were fewer of them, and that the artillery's organization within the Army of Northern Virginia made it difficult to shift batteries effectively. Nevertheless, Confederates inflicted much damage with their artillery, especially when it was deployed at close range.

Edward P. Alexander, commander of artillery in Longstreet's corps, described a particularly fierce artillery duel with Union gunners in the Peach Orchard: "At close range there was less inequality in our guns, and especially our ammunition, and I thought that if ever I could overwhelm and crush them then I would do it now. But they really surprised me, both with the number of guns they developed, and how they stuck to them. I don't think there was ever in our war a hotter, harder, sharper artillery afternoon than this."

A Peach Orchard Became the Center of Bloody Fighting

Daniel Sickles' repositioned line made a V, with the point on the relatively high ground of Sherfy's Peach Orchard along the Emmitsburg Road. The line's right ran northeast along the road; the left extended southeast through rolling fields and woods to a jumble of huge boulders known as Devil's Den.

With the attack under way, one of Longstreet's foremost objectives was to take the orchard, which was a keystone of the Union line. The fighting there was terrific, and losses on both sides were great. Union soldier Frank Haskell described the action: "Upon the front and right flank of Sickles came sweeping the infantry of Longstreet and Hill. Hitherto there had been skirmishing and artillery practice—now the battle began; for amid the heavier smoke and larger tongues of flame of the batteries, now began to appear the countless flashes and the long fiery sheets of the muskets, and the rattle of volleys mingles with the thunder of the guns.

"We see the long gray lines come sweeping down upon Sickles' front, and mix with the battle smoke; now the same colors emerge from the bushes and orchards upon the right, and envelope his flank in the confusion of the conflict."

In the midst of the carnage, an elderly farmer named James Wentz waited out the battle in the cellar of his small cottage, the foundation of which is still visible today. He emerged unharmed when the fighting ended. Hours earlier, his son, whom he had not seen in twenty-four years, had been fighting alongside the Washington Battery of New Orleans in the house's front yard.

Lincoln Offered Sickles Comfort

After the battle, Sickles faced harsh criticism for his actions on July 2, and he never stopped trying to clear his name. In these efforts, he obtained a powerful supporter. President Lincoln, responding to the general's request for a formal review of his decisions at Gettysburg, had these words for the beleaguered commander: "They say you pushed your men out too near the enemy, and began the fight just as that council [Meade's strategy session] was about to meet, at three o'clock in the afternoon of the battle. I am afraid what they say is true, and God bless you for it. Don't ask us to order an inquest to relieve you from bringing on the battle of Gettysburg.

History will set you all right and give everybody his just place, and there is glory enough to go all round."

Historians believe that the president, frustrated with what he thought was an excess of caution in the Union command, appreciated Sickles' boldness at Gettysburg.

A Wheatfield Became a "Maelstrom of Death"

Between the Peach Orchard and Devil's Den lay a wheatfield, over which regiments from five different corps fought doggedly to gain the upper hand. Hour after hour the battle raged, until the earth oozed blood and the brooks ran red. Six times Confederates captured the field and six times they were driven back by fierce counterattacks. The grounds were covered with dead and wounded, blue and gray alike—five hundred Confederate dead were later found within the confines of the small field. The place was often described as a whirlpool, a maelstrom of death, because of the way regiment after regiment was sucked into its vortex and destroyed.

An Irish Chaplain Offered Absolution

Union colonel Patrick Kelly led the "Irish Brigade," comprising regiments from New York, Massachusetts, and Pennsylvania. Many of the men in these units were Irish Catholics from cities in the North. In the midst of the second day's battle, the brigade was sent to join the fight for the Wheatfield. As they were assembled, the brigade's chaplain, the Reverend William Corby, asked for permission to address the men. He stood on a boulder and reminded the troops that cowardice and disloyalty in battle would prevent them from receiving a Christian burial if they were killed. He then offered a general absolution, asking the men to confess their sins as soon as they could. The brief ceremony created long-lasting memories for many of the participants. Corps commander Winfield Scott Hancock, who watched the gathering, was notably moved. In the

Wheatfield, almost 200 of the Irish Brigade's 530 members were killed or wounded. One observer wrote that as the men prayed, many of them were doing so "in their burial clothes."

A statue of Father Corby now stands on Cemetery Ridge; it's the only monument to a chaplain on the field. An identical monument stands on the campus of the University of Notre Dame, where Corby served as president after the war.

A Hound Honors Its Irish Masters

The size of the Irish Brigade was greatly reduced at Fredericksburg and Chancellorsville and the unit entered the fighting at Gettysburg severly understrength. As part of John Caldwell's division, it saw hard action in the Wheatfield. The brigade's Gettysburg monument, dedicated in 1888, is one of the most distinctive in the park. It features at its base a life-size Irish wolfhound mourning its missing masters.

Fighting Raged Over Devil's Den

As it did in the Wheatfield, control of Devil's Den swung back and forth throughout the second day. Hundreds of soldiers swarmed over its boulders; some of the killed and wounded slipped into crevices and remained hidden for days. A small clearing just south of the boulders saw particularly heavy fighting and became known as the Slaughter Pen. It wasn't until six in the evening that Federal defenders, under attack from the west and the south, finally gave way. The Confederates moved in, planting their flags on the den's topmost rocks. Although sharpshooters used Devil's Den to pick off troops on Little Round Top, the site didn't figure in the fighting for the rest of the battle.

Protecting the Colors Was of Great Importance

Preventing the capture of the unit's flag was of great importance to a Civil War soldier. One Union color sergeant, Harvey Munsell, described how he accomplished this after being driven from Devil's Den: "I retreated with the flag a few hundred yards in good order, but shortly a shell came whizzing past, then another, and still another, bursting all around me. One struck the ground, tearing it up, and burst right at my feet. Stunned by the concussion, I tumbled into the depression it made, and many of our men, who looked back and saw me fall, reported me dead: 'Munsell all blown to atoms by a shell, and the flag captured.' That both the flag and myself were not captured was no fault of mine, for there we were for a long time, playing possum, and I apparently dead as Julius Caesar. The staff laid along the surface of the ground in my front, under some rocks and bushes; the flag under my body, with my feet and legs out, as a wounded or dead man would naturally lie, stretched at full length . . . I dared not move from that position until the coast was clear to the rear; the only thing I feared was that a Johnnie might come along and try his bayonet on me to see if I was really dead.

"Just about that time the 6th Corps swept down toward and past me, driving every reb before it. I jumped up and skedaddled to the rear, where my regiment had formed, and quietly fell into line and unfurled the flag. Such a shouting I never heard before or since."

Generals Gave Sometimes-Baffling Orders

A Union soldier positioned along the Emmitsburg Road remembered waiting for the Rebel attack: "The skirmishers fell back to the main line, which was calmly resting in the road and holding its fire until the rebels should reach and attempt to climb a rail fence in front. The regular battery, planted upon the left of the regiment, decimated their ranks with terrible discharges of canister that swept the field again and again and caused clouds of dust; and all thought that the repulse might be decisive."

He was dismayed, however, when the seemingly well-placed line was ordered to alter its position in the face of the enemy. "Before our regiment could deliver its volley, the companies about-faced in pursuance of the orders of some stupid general, and executed a right half-wheel under a severe fire . . . and thus abandoned the advantages of a strong line of defense in the road."

It Was the Worst Time to Be a Soldier

The Civil War was the worst time to be a soldier because military technology had outpaced military tactics. The standard infantry strategy of the time was to march massed foot soldiers two lines deep, shoulder to shoulder, in successive waves against the enemy position. Once they got within one hundred yards, they would fire a volley and then attack the position by charging, relying on brute force and overwhelming numbers to win the day. This tactic had worked well with the weaponry of previous wars. The old smooth-bore musket was effective to only one hundred yards, and artillery was usually solid shot.

By the time of the Civil War, however, the rifled musket and conical minie ball were deadly at five hundred yards, and artillery used exploding shells with a range of almost a mile. This meant that advancing troops came under deadly fire before they ever got within charging distance.

Meade Picked a Perfect Spot for His Headquarters

When Meade reached the battlefield he set up headquarters in a small, whitewashed farmhouse just off the Taneytown Road, which entered Gettysburg from the southeast. The building stood a few hundred yards east of what became known as the Angle, just behind the crest of Cemetery Ridge in the center of the Union line.

Even though the building was not well protected—spent rifle balls and unspent artillery missiles could and did strike the house during the battle—it was an ideal spot for quick and easy contact with all parts of the Federal line and reserves. From the farmhouse, with its stone-floored patio covered by a grape arbor, Meade was able to direct so successfully the rapid shift of brigades and divisions, both infantry and artillery, the frenzied fighting at Gettysburg required him to.

Big Round Top Offered an Unused Advantage

On the far right of the Confederate line were troops led by William Oates. As his men moved forward to attack the Union left on the second day, they found themselves having to go over Big Round Top, a high prominence just southwest of the Federal position. The climb was steep, and at times the men had to pull themselves up by shrubs on the rocky slope, all while being targeted by enemy sharpshooters. When at last they reached the summit, Oates remembered, "some of my men fainted from heat, exhaustion, and thirst. I halted and let them lie down and rest a few minutes."

The hilltop offered a spectacular view of the battlefield. "I saw Gettysburg through the foliage of the trees," Oates wrote. "Saw the smoke and heard the roar of battle which was then raging at the Devil's Den, in the Peach Orchard, up the Emmitsburg Road, and on the west and south of Little Round Top."

The general thought that Big Round Top, which was higher than the adjacent Little Round Top, would offer an almost unassailable position from which to harass the Union line with artillery fire. But his orders were to attack the Federals below, and so after a brief, animated conversation with his commander's adjutant, Oates led his men down the opposite side of the hill into the face of the Union line.

Little Round Top Was Defended in the Nick of Time

In the midst of the second day's battle, Meade's chief engineer, Gouverneur Warren, made a reconnaissance trip to Little Round Top, which marked the southern end of Cemetery Ridge. He was shocked to find it virtually unoccupied. In the distance, he could see Longstreet's corps fast approaching the hill, around the far left of Sickles' line, which until that morning had been positioned on the ridge.

Seeing immediately the danger to the Union flank, Warren dashed off to find whatever troops he could to protect Little Round Top. He grabbed a brigade led by Strong Vincent and sent them off at a run to the top of the hill. As they reached the crest, they saw a Confederate brigade just starting to climb the other side.

Vincent's men charged and threw the Confederates backward. A second Union brigade entered the fray as Confederate reinforcements arrived. In the midst of hand-to-hand combat, two Union cannons reached the crest and poured a destructive fire into the Confederate ranks. The fight lasted for some time, but the Federals did not yield, despite losing three generals, who died protecting the heights. Had Little Round Top fallen into Confederate hands, the whole of Meade's Gettysburg force could well have been lost.

The Hill Gave Its Defenders Natural Protection

A Confederate private remembered attacking Union troops on Little Round Top: "There was a long line of large boulders cropping out on the mountainside, forming a natural breastwork. Over and through this the line had to mount. The line became broken because of the timber, and those of us in the front line, as soon as we were uncovered, received the first fire of the hidden Federals. A long line of us went down, three of us close together. There was a sharp, electric pain in the lower part of the body, and then a sinking sensation to the earth; and, falling, all things growing dark, the one and last idea passing through the mind was, 'This is the last of earth.'

"Over their fallen comrades the men rushed up the mountainside, and soon struck the main line of the enemy, for there was a crash of musketry at close range. Minie balls were falling through the leaves like hail in a thunderstorm. Consciousness had returned. Dragging himself along the stony earth, as a wounded snake might have done, this soldier took shelter under a boulder."

A Professor Became a War Hero

At the very left of the line of defenders sent to protect Little Round Top was the 20th Maine regiment, led by Joshua Chamberlain, who had quit his job as a professor at Bowdoin College to join the army. Ordered to hold its position "at all costs," the regiment fought off repeated attacks until, as one participant remembered, "the blood stood in puddles in some places on the rocks" and the soldiers were nearly out of ammunition. They then fixed bayonets, launched a desperate charge, took many prisoners, and drove the Confederates into a retreat.

Chamberlain was hailed as a hero, and the regiment's actions at Gettysburg became legendary. When he was discharged from the army after the war, Chamberlain returned to Bowdoin, but education was no longer the career he wanted to pursue. Military life had changed him. "In the privations and sufferings endured as well as in the strenuous action of battle," he wrote, "some of the highest qualities of manhood are called forth—courage, self-command, sacrifice of self for the sake of something held higher."

Chamberlain was recruited to run for governor of Maine; he was elected and served four terms. He then became president of Bowdoin. But he would never again achieve the success and fulfillment he found during the Gettysburg campaign.

Chamberlain Was on the Verge of Defeat

In his July 6 report on the action at Little Round Top, Chamberlain described in detail just how close his men were to defeat as they struggled to hold off the Rebel attack: "It did not seem possible to withstand another shock like this now coming on. Our loss had been severe. One-half of my left wing had fallen, and a third of my regiment lay just behind us, dead or badly wounded. . . . It was imperative to strike before we were struck by this overwhelming force in a hand-to-hand fight, which we could not probably have withstood or survived. At that crisis, I ordered the bayonet. The word was enough. It ran like fire along the line, from man to man, and rose into a shout, with which they sprang upon the enemy, now not 30 yards away. The effect was surprising; many of the enemy's first line threw down their arms and surrendered."

Chamberlain Ordered a Salute at Appomattox

In April 1865, Joshua Chamberlain was detailed to command Union troops who received the ceremonial surrender of Lee's infantry at Appomattox Court House. The momentous meaning of the occasion, he said later, impressed him deeply. He thought the defeated soldiers deserved some recognition, not only for their valor at arms, but as a welcome back into the Union. On his own authority, "well aware of the responsibility assumed and of the criticism that would follow," he ordered that as each Confederate division came up to stack its arms and lay down its colors, a bugle be sounded and the whole Union line from right to left come to "shouldered arms," a position requiring steadiness and silence and denoting respect.

Civilians Had a Bird's-Eye View

The highest point in the region, Indian Lookout, near Emmitsburg, Maryland, offered civilians a bird's-eye view of the events unfolding at Gettysburg, some ten miles to the northeast. One wartime observer wrote that there were people on the lookout "almost the whole time during the three days.

"We had plenty of glasses viz telescopes, spy, and opera glasses. We had a clear view of the field and could see so as to make out the men in their lines, attending cannons, the cannons themselves, making charges, officers riding along their lines, and in a word the whole scene was spread out to our view. . . . We could distinctly observe the changes in the position of the armies: sometimes one army would slowly give way, but seeming to dispute every inch of ground."

Barksdale Led a "Magnificent" Charge

"The most magnificent charge of the war," as one observer called it, was made through the Peach Orchard by a Mississippi brigade. On July 2 at six o'clock, Confederate troops led by William Barksdale stepped off from Seminary Ridge and moved rapidly across the field. They swept past the Sherfy farm buildings and on through the orchard's trees. Union troops and cannons blazed away, attempting to stop the attack, but the Confederates returned fire, and the defenders melted away. Barksdale himself, his long white hair flying, led his men across the Emmitsburg Road, then turned them left to roll up the Federal line.

In his wake, another Confederate unit quickly swept through the orchard and headed toward the Wheatfield. The Union brigade trying to stop the Mississippi onslaught retreated in disarray, heading back toward Cemetery Ridge; it had lost almost half its men. Barksdale's momentum carried him into the valley in front of the rise, where reinforcing fire finally forced him to halt. The general was hit and mortally wounded, his body recovered the next day.

Federals on Culp's Hill Thought the Army Had Been Outmaneuvered

On July 2, Union soldier Van Willard, who wrote extensively about army life, was with the 3rd Wisconsin on Culp's Hill, out of the action there. He described hearing the sounds of the fighting at Little Round Top, the Peach Orchard, and Cemetery Ridge in the distance: "Late in the day (three in the afternoon, or perhaps a little after) we were startled by the heavy booming of cannon far around to the left of the horseshoe like line that had been formed. The firing was almost opposite in direction from that in which we were looking for the enemy, and at that time we supposed the Rebels had gone around to our rear, as they had done at Chancellorsville.

"Gun followed gun, roar after roar, so rapidly that when our batteries opened in return the cannonading became one continuous roar. . . . After an hour and a half of this terrible uproar, it began suddenly to die away, and soon only a few batteries were in play and there were brief intervals between the discharges. But there came up to us the 'still small voice' of musketry, still and small it seemed compared with the cannonading, yet we well knew that there was more death in that voice than in the thunder tones of the artillery."

The South Briefly Gained Cemetery Ridge

At one point during the second day's fighting, Confederate troops managed to breach the Union line on Cemetery Ridge. A brigade led by Ambrose R. Wright had charged across the Emmitsburg Road north of the Peach Orchard, shattering each line it encountered. "We were now," remembered Wright, "within less than 100 yards of the crest of the heights, which were lined by artillery, supported by a strong body of infantry, under protection of a stone fence. My men, by a well-directed fire, soon drove the cannoneers from their guns, and, leaping over the fence, charged up to the top of the crest and drove the enemy's infantry. . . .

"We were now completely masters of the field, having gained the key, as it were, of the enemy's whole line. Unfortunately, just as we had carried the enemy's last and strongest position it was discovered that the brigade on our right had not only not advanced across the turnpike, but had given way and were rapidly falling back to the rear, while on our left we were entirely unprotected, the brigade ordered to our support having failed to advance." Reluctantly, Wright was forced to withdraw. As he did, Union troops regained their cannons and fired into the retreating ranks with deadly effect.

Nightfall Helped the Union on Culp's Hill

Throughout July 2, Union troops on Culp's Hill put in long hours scraping up loose dirt and rocks to make a low beastworks, in some spots using logs and fence rails to strengthen the line. A division led by James Wadsworth occupied the western crest facing the town and Cemetery Hill, but supporting divisions had been pulled to join the fighting on the far left of the Federal line. The entire eastern face of Culp's Hill was barren of defenders.

To fill the gap, sixty-three-year-old general George Greene stretched his small brigade to the east of Wadsworth's men, then angled his line sharply to the south. When Confederate troops attacked that evening, Greene's shrewd positioning helped the Union hold the hill against superior numbers for some two hours, until Greene had to call on Wadsworth for support. Even with the help, however, Confederates gradually broke through to occupy abandoned Union trenches in the growing darkness. But night fighting has never been particularly attractive to soldiers or their officers. Targets cannot be seen, and the landscape looks different than it actually is. As though by common consent, the firing ceased, with both sides content to wait for daylight to renew the struggle.

For the Confederates, this was an unfortunate occurrence. Without knowing it, they had fought to within a few hundred yards of the Baltimore Pike, Meade's lifeline to Baltimore and Washington, and squarely in the Union's right flank and rear. But they didn't press their advantage.

Attack Orders Were Seen as "Murder"

Although the Confederate attack on Culp's Hill was made without a supporting attack on any other part of the Union line, the bitter fighting lasted for hours and took a huge toll on both sides. At one point, when the Confederates seemed to be withdrawing, two Union regiments were ordered to make a bold charge across an open field. The commander of one of these regiments, Charles Mudge, could not believe that such an order would be made and asked for clarification. The order was repeated, and Mudge dutifully complied, remarking, "it's murder, but it's an order." He led his troops forward, and when they reached the middle of the field, hidden Confederates opened fire, decimating the attackers and forcing a hasty retreat. Among the dead was Mudge.

Enemies Could Be Merciful to Each Other

A Union private remembered laying wounded in the darkness near enemy lines: "There I was all night with none but the dead, save now and then a ghoul in gray searching the dead and stripping them of clothes. If seen by our pickets they were fired on and driven away. The night was long and dark to me. I thought, if the boys could, they would come for me.

"Toward morning a man in gray came near me. He appeared to be looking about, but not trying to strip any bodies. He stood looking at me, and I put out my hand to touch his foot. He jumped as if surprised; he probably thought me dead. On recovering, he stooped over, asked me where I was shot, if I was cold, and got a rubber blanket, placed it under me, and covered me with two of woolen. He sat by me some time, talking, till it began to be light, then gave me his canteen of water, saying he must get back to his post."

Ten Top Generals Were Wounded, One Killed

During the fighting, five Union corps or division commanders were wounded (Hancock, Sickles, Gibbon, Birney, and Barlow) and five Confederate corps or division commanders were wounded (Hood, Heth, Pettigrew, Pender, and Trimble). One corps or division commander was killed: John Reynolds. At the brigade level, many more generals were injured or lost.

A Private Relief Agency Worked Wonders

During the second day of the battle, when Union medical personnel were already feeling the effects of orders to hold supply trains far to the rear, two wagons appeared on Cemetery Ridge with the inscription "U.S. San. Com." on their sides. A surgeon working nearby, surrounded by the wounded, exclaimed when he noticed the vehicles, "Thank God, here comes the Sanitary Commission. Now we shall be able to do something." His excitement was justified. Both wagons were filled with sponges, chloroform, beef soup, brandy, lint, bandages, and many other badly needed items.

It was just one more instance of this unique relief organization being on hand when and where it was needed most. The United States Sanitary Commission was known to demonstrate a system and planning that often put government providers to shame.

If ever the name of an agency was misleading as to its actual function, it was that of the Sanitary Commission. The official connection of this private enterprise with the national government was merely the authority it had been given by Congress to report upon the state of sanitation at army camps and hospitals. But the organizers of the service had managed to expand its influence to a point where, a mere two years after its formation, it had become a catalyst for more than seven thousand relief organizations throughout the country. The organization channeled its donations of everything from books to blankets to the troops on such a massive scale it was sometimes difficult to discern which was the army's primary supplier, the government or the commission.

Sharpshooters Commandeered Homes

While most of the battle happened on land surrounding Gettysburg, the town itself was not spared much danger. In fact, after the first day, some of the southern and eastern parts of town were an active part of the Confederate line. Streets here were barricaded, and the windows of upstairs windows bristled with sharpshooters harassing the Federals on Cemetery Hill. At least one section of row houses had been subjected to a unique improvisation: passageways were cut through the upstairs walls so the Rebels could easily pass from one house to another.

Sharpshooters posed a threat to civilians, as related by one resident at the time: "Our house stood on the corner of Baltimore and High Streets, and we did not dare to look out of the windows on the Baltimore Street side. Sharpshooters from Cemetery Hill were watching all the houses for Confederate sharpshooters, and from that distance they could not distinguish citizen from soldier."

Lee's "Eyes and Ears" Arrived Late

On the night of July 2, Confederate cavalry commander J. E. B. Stuart made his long-delayed appearance at Lee's headquarters. He and his men were absent during the first two days of fighting, and Lee was left to operate without the vital intelligence that a mobile cavalry can provide.

When Stuart arrived, Lee raised his hand in a questioning gesture, asking, "General Stuart, where have you been? I have not heard a word from you for days, and you are the eyes and ears of my army." According to one witness, Stuart "wilted" at this question, explaining that he had spent his time capturing 150 enemy wagons, among other things. Lee didn't press his point, however, telling Stuart that he needed his help now.

Lee Was Ill During Much of the Battle

When Confederate captain William Blackford reported to Lee's tent in the morning of July 2 he was told that he would not be able to meet with the general. Instead, he was to give his report to an officer who would pass it along to Lee. Blackford later wrote that as he talked with the officer, he was surprised to see Lee "come out of his tent and go to the rear several times while I was there and he walked so much as if he was weak and in pain that I asked one of the gentlemen present what was the matter with him, and he told me General Lee was suffering a good deal from an attack of diarrhea."

After the war, John Gordon noted that Lee's "nearest approach to fault-finding" regarding Gettysburg "was his statement that his own sight was not perfect, and that he was so dull that, in attempting to use the eyes of others, he found himself often misled."

Some historians believe that during the Battle of Gettysburg Lee was self-medicating with quinine, which is known to cause ringing in the head and ears, muscular weakness, severe bowel trouble, and disturbed vision. He had used it before. In April 1863, when Lee was confined to bed with a sharp pain in his chest, back, and arms, he wrote "my head is ringing with quinine & I am otherwise so poorly I do not seem able to think." That attack, at first thought to be rheumatism, was the forerunner of the heart condition that led to his death in 1870.

A Soldier's Fare Was Meager

As might be imagined, the average Civil War soldier was often hungry, and when he did eat, the fare was meager. The Union's dietary staple was hardtack—baked biscuits of flour, salt, and water. These were easy to transport and hard enough to hold up when shipped. They were so hard, in fact, that soldiers had to bash them into bits with rocks or rifle butts or soak them to make them edible. Confederate troops relied on cornmeal, which was fried in grease to make what were called "Johnnie Cakes." Meat—usually salted bacon, beef, or pork—was hard to come by and often spoiled or inedible because of preservatives. Implements to cook meat were also in short supply.

Rice and dried beans were sometimes available (the Southerners had peanuts and dried peas, too), as were "dessicated" vegetables. Union soldiers had condensed milk (newly invented), tea, or coffee.

Confederates made do without coffee—it was blocked from Southern ports—and so brewed a substitute from chicory, dried apples, dried beans, acorns, or whatever else seemed like it might work.

A War Artist Drew What He Saw

Some of the most memorable images of the battle were captured by Alfred Waud, a war artist for *Harper's Weekly,* the most popular periodical of the day. Born in London, Waud arrived in New York in 1850 and worked as a stage painter and illustrator. When war broke out, he traveled across the theater of battle, observing the fighting and life behind the lines. He drew pencil or ink sketches of what he saw, and these were rushed by mail or courier to New York engravers, who made reproducible wood-block etchings from the art for publication—the whole process took from three to four weeks. Waud was respected by soldiers and fellow artists alike. A colleague wrote that he had "total disregard for personal safety and comfort, an owl-like propensity to sit up all night and a hawky style of vigilance during the day."

The Third Day

Longstreet Opposed Lee's Plan for the Final Assault

On the morning of July 3, Lee selected as his next point of attack what he believed to be the weakest point of the Union line arrayed along Cemetery Ridge—the troops in the center. He reasoned that an attack made at this point could be hit from the side only by the guns on Little Round Top, on the Union left, and these, he believed, could be silenced by his own artillery. A successful attack on the center would split the entire Union line, and this is what Lee proposed to do.

Longstreet was directed to have a division commanded by George Pickett lead the assault. Attached to Pickett's division were a number of other brigades so that the attacking force would be some fifteen thousand strong.

Longstreet opposed Lee's plan for a number of reasons. "I thought that it would not do," he wrote, "that the point had been fully tested the day before by more men, when all were fresh; that the enemy was there looking for us . . . that thirty thousand men was the minimum of force necessary for the work . . . that a column would have to march a mile under concentrated battery fire, and a thousand yards under long-range musketry. . . . Opinion was then expressed that the fifteen thousand men who could make a successful assault over that field had never been arrayed for battle; but [Lee] was impatient of listening and tired of talking and nothing was left but to proceed."

Pickett's Men Were the Last to Arrive

When Confederate troops rushed to Gettysburg on the battle's first day, George Pickett's division was ordered to remain near Chambersburg to guard the army's rear. It wasn't until the next morning that Pickett's men were put on the road to join the fighting. When they reached Gettysburg that afternoon after a hard march, some historians believe Longstreet asked Pickett to send them in immediately to join the fray and that Pickett protested, saying his men were too exhausted. Lee himself was reportedly relieved when Pickett's division finally reached the field. When he saw the general in person, Lee promised him "I shall have work for you tomorrow."

Although the division commanded by Pickett led the assault on the Union center, it wasn't the only division to make the charge. The attack plan called for two brigades from Richard Anderson's division to advance on Pickett's right. A division led by James Pettigrew was to advance on Pickett's left. And two brigades from Isaac Trimble's division were to follow behind Pettigrew.

Meade Predicted the Attack's Target

On the evening of July 2, Meade held a council of war with his top commanders. After discussion and voting, the group settled on a strategy: to wait in a defensive posture until Lee either attacked or moved. Union general John Gibbon, whose troops were in the middle of Cemetery Ridge, was part of the meeting. Gibbon remembered that "as the council broke up, Meade said to me, 'If Lee attacks tomorrow, it will be in your front.' I asked him why he thought so and he replied, 'Because he has made attacks on both our flanks and failed and if he concludes to try it again, it will be on our centre.' I expressed a hope that he would and told Gen. Meade with confidence that if he did, we would defeat him.

"Meade's reliance upon the doctrine of chances, that having tried each of our wings, Lee would, if he made a third trial, make it upon our centre, struck me as somewhat remarkable. But he was right."

An Eyewitness Gave Vivid Descriptions of Generals

Sensing that the meeting of Federal commanders at Meade's headquarters the night of July 2 was a momentous occasion, Frank Haskell, an aide to Gibbon, took careful note of the participants and later described them in detail in a letter to his brother:

Sedgwick: "A heavy man, short, thick-set, and muscular, with florid complexion. . . . He has a magnificent profile, well cut, with the nose and forehead forming almost a straight line."

Alfred Pleasonton, commander of the Cavalry Corps: "Quite a nice little dandy, with brown hair and beard, straw hat with a little jockey rim, which he cocks upon one side of his head."

Meade: "A tall, spare man, with full beard, which with his hair, originally brown, is quite thickly sprinkled with gray—has a Roman-ish face, very large nose, and white, large forehead. . . . His habitual personal appearance is quite careless, and it would be difficult to make him look well dressed."

Hancock: "The tallest and most shapely, and in many respects the best looking officer of them all. . . . Features neither large nor small, but well cut, with full jaw and chin, compressed mouth, straight nose, full, deep blue eyes, and a very mobile, emotional countenance. He always dressed remarkably well. And his manner is dignified, gentlemanly, and commanding. I think that if he were in citizens' clothes, and should give commands in the army to those who did not know him, he would be likely to be obeyed at once, and without question as to his right to command."

Warren Earned His Rest

Chief engineer Gouverneur Warren consulted with Meade throughout the battle and helped spearhead the defense of Little Round Top on July 2. But he was exhausted by nightfall and dozed off during the commander's famous council of war. Meade decided to let him sleep.

A Lengthy Assault Died Out on Culp's Hill

The first attack on July 3 was made by Union artillery on Culp's Hill. At daybreak, some two dozen cannons began pounding the positions Confederate soldiers had gained the evening before. Under the shelling, Confederate general Edward Johnson prepared his brigades for a direct assault on the hill, although one of his commanders later wrote that the Union line there "could not have been carried by any force." The attack commenced, but it stalled under heavy fire. Johnson was hoping the coordinated attack he thought was coming from Longstreet's troops would soon draw defenders away from Culp's Hill. And so he ordered another advance; it too stalled with heavy losses.

At 10 AM, after some five hours of intense fighting, Johnson ordered a third assault, unaware that Pickett's attack on the Union center would not be happening anytime soon. Like the ones before it, this third assault failed. "Flesh and blood could not live in such a fire," an attacker wrote later. Johnson finally retreated, and for the rest of the battle, the Union's right flank was secure.

The Union Cavalry Got Better

The Confederate cavalry was widely seen as being vastly superior to its Northern counterpart at the start of the war. Riding was a popular Southern pastime in the years leading up to the conflict, but the average Federal cavalryman started service with little or no riding experience. Still, the Union cavalry was quite effective throughout the Gettysburg Campaign, holding its own against a highly skilled enemy. Historians note that the battle corresponded with a turning point in the relative strengths of the mounted units. A member of Stuart's staff said as much after the war: "During the last two years no branch of the Army of the Potomac contributed so much to the overthrow of Lee's army as the cavalry."

Why did the Southern cavalry seem to weaken compared to the Union's? Stuart's staffer gave one reason: The Confederate government, he said, "committed the fatal error of allowing the men to muster their own horses, paying them a per diem for their use, and the muster valuation in cases whether they were killed in action, but giving no compensation for horses lost by any other casualties of a campaign. . . . Toward the close of the war many were unable to remount themselves, and hundreds of such dismounted men were collected in a useless crowd, which was dubbed 'Company Q.'"

General Custer Made His Debut

All during the Battle of Gettysburg, cavalry units from both armies were busy along the perimeter of the field, probing enemy positions, protecting supply lines, and occasionally engaging in fierce firefights. In the afternoon of the third day, Confederate cavalry troops attacked their Union counterparts a few miles east of the front lines. The duel grew in intensity, as the Southerners stubbornly pressed ahead. One Union mounted brigade in particular helped blunt the assault by attacking the enemy head on. It was commanded by a general dressed in an outlandish costume—black jackboots, olive breeches, a tight black jacket trimmed with silver, a red scarf, and a rakish hat—his long hair in ringlets scented with spice. The man was George Armstrong Custer, leading troops in combat for the very first time.

The Field Was Vast and Exposed

One of Pickett's men described the setting of the final grand charge as he surveyed the Union position on Cemetery Ridge from across a vast, sloping field: "A loose stone-fence or wall, common in the country, ran along the side of this ridge, offering cover and protection to his infantry, while a common rail-fence running through the bottom land presented an obstacle to the advance of our men. From the crest of the hill, where our men first became exposed to the direct fire, down the descent, and up to the enemy's front must have been, I should think, half a mile, at least, of entirely open and exposed ground. Over this terrible space, within canister and shrap-nel range, it would be necessary for our brave and devoted boys to go, before striking the foe at anything like close quarters.

"It looked—even in that morning's light, before a deadly shot had been fired, before a drop of blood had spotted that green meadow, which was soon to be soaked with bloody carnage . . . like a passage to the valley of death."

The Attack Began with an Earthshaking Barrage

At 1:07 PM on July 3, the world seemed to explode for the soldiers on Cemetery Ridge. In response to two signal guns in the Peach Orchard, all 140 Confederate fieldpieces opened with solid shot and shell. Union artillery quickly responded, and the roar of more than 200 guns ushered in the most stupendous artillery duel ever fought on American soil. One Northerner later wrote, "The air was full of grass and dirt cast from the soil by the jagged rebel iron. . . . There seemed to be no place where they did not strike and no spot from whence they did not come."

When the bombardment began, the infantrymen on Cemetery Ridge grabbed their muskets and rushed forward to positions behind stone walls and rail fences about a hundred yards beyond the crest of the hillside. As a result, they suffered little damage because the Confederate gunners were aiming too high. Others, particularly the support troops and officers behind the front lines, were not as fortunate. Meade's headquarters were at the center of the impact area. Although none of Meade's staff officers was hit, sixteen horses were killed. The whole outfit quickly moved out of range to nearby Power's Hill.

The Guns Were Heard Near Pittsburgh

Unbelievably, people near Pittsburgh, Pennsylvania, claimed they heard the great Gettysburg cannonade, even though they were located some 150 miles away. Could this be possible? Experts in acoustics say that, while extremely improbable, such a phenomenon could, in theory, occur. When a large gun is fired, most of the sound waves are projected up into the air, where they are continually refracted upward so they never descend. The waves that are heard are those that stay close to earth. But differences in air temperature, favorable winds, and reflection from dense air strata could cause sound waves to bend back downward after they've traveled a great distance, perhaps even a hundred miles or more.

Firing a Cannon Required a Well-Trained Team

In ideal circumstances, the artillerymen at each cannon positioned on the battlefield followed a well-choreographed procedure to fire a big gun. In battle, each individual had a specific duty: one would insert the charge and projectile into the muzzle, one would swab the bore and ram the load, one would operate the cannon's vent, one would prime and fire the piece, and so on. A gunner, usually a corporal, at each cannon would make sure it was properly aimed—adjusting the height by twisting the screw under the barrel or having the gun moved to one side or the other by its tail—and give the signal to fire. Each artilleryman knew how to perform all the tasks needed to fire the gun—which was necessary because in the heat of an artillery duel, or when the team was under fire, the procedure would understandably break down and have to change as men were hit and gear was damaged.

The Union Used Artillery More Effectively

One of the key differences between the armies during most of the Civil War—and certainly at Gettysburg—was their use of artillery. A Union private observed that "there is one thing that our government does that suits me to a dot. That is, we fight mostly with artillery. The rebels fight mostly with infantry."

Much of the truth in that statement is because of Union general Henry Hunt, one of the few men of rank on either side to fully understand, and have the ability to implement, the full capabilities of the artillery. He concentrated several batteries together on key features of the terrain to maximize their firepower against attack at any point.

At Gettysburg, Hunt formed his guns into two lines of forty to fifty guns each, one south of the trees on Cemetery Ridge, one on Cemetery Hill, with a commanding view of the entire field. He saw to it that ammunition and the guns held in reserve were well placed and readily available. As commander of the Federal artillery during the battle, Hunt was one of the great unsung Union heroes.

The Cannonade Lasted Longer Than Planned

Edward Porter Alexander, in charge of the Confederate cannonade, thought the artillery assault would last only ten or fifteen minutes, but because return fire was so intense, he continued the barrage for an hour and a half. Worried that his ammunition was being depleted, he sent a message to Pickett as soon as the enemy fire seemed to slacken: "For God's sake, come quick!"

A Nod Began the Charge

When Pickett received Alexander's message, he asked Longstreet if he should begin the charge. The corps commander was still not convinced the attack could succeed, but he knew Lee was committed to moving forward. "My feelings had so overcome me that I could not speak," Longstreet would later write, "for fear of betraying my want of confidence to him." Longstreet merely nodded his head, and the order to advance was given.

Pickett Rallied His Men

A Confederate officer hit during the cannonade remembered when he heard the order to move out. "As the artillery fire had practically ceased," he wrote, "there came the order, 'Fall in!' and brave General Pickett, coming close to where I lay wounded, called out: 'Up, men, and to your posts! Don't forget that you are from old Virginia!' The effect of this word upon the men was electrical. The regiments were quickly in line, closing to the left over the dead and wounded—the ranks now reduced by the losses occasioned by the shelling to about 4,400 men of the division, and I am satisfied that Kemper's brigade, the smallest of the division, did not then number over 1,250.

"The advance now began, the men calling out to the wounded and others: 'Goodbye, boys! Goodbye!'"

The Initial Advance Was a Spectacle

After the artillery fire stopped, the battlefield grew strangely silent. As the long gray infantry lines emerged from the center of the woods on Seminary Ridge, every eye focused on the amazing scene. Some units marched with their rifles at the right shoulder; others carried them at trail or in the position of a hunting piece. The lines marched as on parade, with colors flying. A few minutes into the march, the men corrected their alignment and moved eastward across the open fields.

A Union officer described the Confederate advance: "Every eye could see his legions, an overwhelming resistless tide of an ocean of armed men sweeping upon us. Regiment after regiment and brigade after brigade move from the woods and rapidly take their places in the lines forming the assault. . . . Barrel and bayonet gleam in the sun, a sloping forest of flashing steel. Right as they move, as with one soul, in perfect order, without impediment of ditch, or wall or stream, over ridge and slope, through orchard and meadow and cornfield, magnificent, grim, irresistible."

The Fog of War Obscured the Objective

For years after the battle, it was believed that a "copse of trees" was the target of Pickett's Charge, which places the final objective of the attack along Cemetery Ridge. But recent examinations of the participants' accounts suggest that winning Cemetery Hill itself might have been the Confederates' true goal.

The collapse of Pickett's right flank during the charge has contributed to the misunderstanding of the event by blurring the purpose, direction, and design of the whole attack. With the shattering of the right and the charge's tendency to dress left toward the division to the north led by Pettigrew, the Confederate attack progressively crowded together in front of the trees on the ridge (which in 1863 would be better described as a clump of bushes). Jumbled and bunched together there, Pickett's men appeared to be focusing solely on that position.

But at the start of the attack, as the Confederate infantry moved forward, with Pickett's division turning forty-five degrees left and continually dressing to connect with the trailing Pettigrew, the charge must have resembled a mile-wide crescent, gradually conforming to the outer circumference of Cemetery Hill. Winfield Scott Hancock, whose corps was defending the ridge, stated that "when the columns of the enemy appeared it looked as if they were going to attack the center of our line, but after marching straight out a little distance they seemed to incline a little to their left, as if their object was to march through my command and seize Cemetery Hill." The testimony of artillery commander Alexander concurred with this belief. "Early in the morning General Lee came around," he stated, "and I was then told to assault Cemetery Hill."

Crossing the Road Hindered the Charge

All the Confederate units involved in the July 3 attack on the Union center had to cross the Emmitsburg Road, and this necessity had an effect on the charge. Cannoneers on Cemetery Ridge knew that crossing the road brought the Rebels within the effective range of canister fire, and so as the attacking troops crossed the road, the defenders switched from cannonball to canister to deadly effect. As well, riflemen on the ridge knew that Rebel troops on the

Union side of the road were now within effective musket range and they could fire with much better accuracy.

For the Confederates, crossing the rail fencing along the road meant that their progress was slowed just as Union gunfire increased dramatically. The need to realign units displaced by the crossing slowed them even more. As well, historians speculate that because the road was slightly sunken, some attackers couldn't resist a last chance to stay put under cover in the midst of a strengthening firestorm.

Armistead Made an Inspirational Showing

A brigade led by Lewis Armistead was in the middle of Pickett's division. When the command came for it to advance, Armistead went out in front of his men to give them their orders, as described by one of the soldiers: "If I should live for a hundred years I shall never forget that moment or the command. . . . He was an old army officer, and was possessed of a very loud voice, which could be heard by the whole brigade, being near my regiment. He gave the command, in words, as follows—'Attention, second battalion! battalion of direction forward; guides center; march!' I never see at any time a battalion of soldiers but what it recalls those words.

"He turned; placed himself about twenty paces in front of his brigade, and took the lead. His place was in the rear, properly. After moving he placed his hat on the point of his sword, and held it above his head, in front of him."

The Canister Was Most Deadly

One of the deadliest pieces of ammunition used during the Battle of Gettysburg was the canister—a container of small iron balls shot from a cannon. When fired, the container would be blown apart and the balls would scatter to hit a large number of men, much as a shotgun blast sprays its payload to deadly effect. On occasion, two canisters were fired at the same time. Also used was grapeshot—

slightly larger iron balls bound with cloth and rope, which would disintegrate upon firing.

Under the order of Henry Hunt, Union cannons were silent when Pickett's lines emerged from the woods and first moved forward. But when the troops crossed the Emmitsburg Road, the artillery opened up—first with solid shot before switching to canister and finally, at point-blank range, to double canister. Under the withering barrage, cohesion between the groups of marching soldiers evaporated. Still they moved forward, disregarding the growing number of dead and wounded who fell away. Perhaps they thought that the sooner they reached the Union defenses and faced mostly musket balls, the greater would be their chances of escaping the artillery fire and coming through with their lives.

Pickett Directed from the Rear

Pickett, on his coal-black horse in the rear of the second line, advanced with his men until the leading wave crossed the Emmitsburg Road. He then halted with his staff and established a field command post near the Codori House, which still stands on the roadside. From there he was in position to direct the final phase of the attack without charging into the Union defenses himself, which division commanders are not supposed to do, according to accepted military practices. When battles reach an advanced stage, there is, in fact, little a division leader can do to influence the events; he can only watch, hope, and send progress reports up the chain of command.

The Right Side Collapsed

Under the pounding of the Federal guns, the Confederate parade formation began to come apart. When the time came to change direction in order to converge on the objective, the two brigades on the right of Pickett's line were slow to conform, with the result that a constantly widening gap developed between them and the rest of the troops.

On the ridge, Union generals spotted the rift and quickly moved to take advantage of it. Three Vermont regiments, "Green Mountain Boys" who had never before seen combat, were thrown into the gap. They first fired northward into the advancing Confederates, who now faced fire from both their front and their flank. Then they turned and directed their attack against the lagging brigades to the south, who, cut off from the main force and now taking unexpected fire from the side, began to beat a bewildered retreat.

The Dead Were Measured "In Yards"

A Union soldier remembered when the advancing Confederates came within rifle range: "Slowly the great line moved forward until it reached the fence. The men mounted to cross when the word fire! fire! ran along the Union line, crack! crack! spoke out the musketry, and the men dropped from the fence as if swept by a gigantic sickle swung by some powerful force of nature. Great gaps were formed in the line, the number of slain and wounded could not be estimated by numbers, but must be measured in yards. . . .

"The men of the regiment still actively continued firing. Several of the men were fortunate in having two breech-loaders for while one was loading the other was firing. So rapid was the firing that the barrels became so hot that it was almost impossible to use them, some using the precious water in their canteens to pour upon the overworked guns."

Two Muzzleloading Rifles Were Common

Two types of rifles were common during the Civil War. The rifle musket Model 1861, known as the Springfield, was a muzzleloading percussion cap rifle with a muzzle opening of a little more than half an inch across—a .58-caliber weapon. It had an effective range of about five hundred yards, weighed nearly ten pounds, and cost the government nineteen dollars each (about seven weeks' pay for a private).

The Enfield musket, Model 1853, imported from England, was also popular. It was a muzzleloader with a caliber of .577, effective to eight hundred yards. It weighed just over nine pounds. Most soldiers thought the Enfield was more accurate than the Springfield.

The Left Fell Just Short

The troops on the left flank of the advancing line received devastating fire when an Ohio regiment found itself able to move out in front of the Federal position and fire into the side of the attackers, just as the Vermont regiments had done so successfully to the south. The toll was high, but enough Confederates withstood this fire to continue their march toward Cemetery Ridge.

Here, however, topography dealt them an unlucky hand. Just north of the copse of trees, the stone wall made a right angle back to the east for one hundred yards or so before angling again to the north. As a result, the Confederates north of the Angle had an extra hundred yards to advance to reach the Union line, and, for this hundred-yard stretch, had to take fire to their side, from behind the portion of the wall that faced north. By the time they crossed this treacherous terrain, only a handful of men were left, and despite a number of valiant attempts, they were unable to penetrate and hold the enemy's line.

The Center Broke the Union Line

Only the Confederate center had strength enough to attack the stone wall in numbers. As the men moved forward, the deadly artillery fire faded away—Union cannons at the Angle were now silent, the men who served the pieces being either wounded or dead. Behind the wall, the Federal infantry waited for the order to fire. Closer and closer came the attackers, to within one hundred yards. Suddenly, the Union line erupted. Sheets of flame spurted from behind the breastworks, where the men were massed three and four deep.

Pausing just long enough to return fire, in the face of repeated Union volleys, the Confederates still on their feet covered the last few yards in a rush. Spurred on by the wild rebel yell, they poured over the wall. In the forefront of the jumbled mass of men and colors was Lewis Armistead, his battered hat still riding on the tip of his sword. When his men made their initial penetration, they drove the Union troops backward, down over the ridge.

Just beyond the stone wall, Armistead placed his free hand on the barrel of a now-silent Union gun, as though to confirm its capture. As he did, he was hit by a hail of gunfire and fell, mortally wounded, to the ground.

The Fighting Was Hand to Hand

Confederate captain J. B. Turney led his men over the wall near the Angle. "At double-quick time, we continued the charge," he remembered, "and not until we were within fifteen steps of the stone wall did I give the command to fire. The volley confused the enemy. I then ordered a charge with bayonets, and on moved our gallant boys. Another instant, and we were engaged in a desperate hand-to-hand conflict for the possession of a fragile wall of masonry that held out as the sole barrier between the combatants.

"Each man seemed to pick his foe, and it fell my lot to struggle with a stalwart Federal officer, who made a vicious thrust at my breast. I parried just in time. Thus for a few moments the contest settled as for a death stuggle, and one triumphant shout was given as the Federals in our immediate front and to our right yielded and fled in confusion to a point just back of the crest of the hill, abandoning their artillery."

Guns Were Used as Clubs

One Union soldier remembered that guns were used as clubs in the frantic fighting. He wrote that a comrade "who was a quite savage sort of fellow, wielded his piece, striking right and left, and was killed in the hell by having his skull crushed by a musket in the hands of a rebel, and Private Donnelly . . . used his piece as a club, and when called upon to surrender replied tauntingly 'I surrender' at the same time striking his would-be captor to the ground."

The Wall Became a Confederate Line of Defense

The stone wall at the Angle was manned by a brigade of Pennsylvanians led by Alexander Webb. One of his officers, Frank Haskell, remembered the tense moments when the attackers broke the Union line, in some cases using the stone wall as their own line of defense.

"Little could be seen of the enemy," he wrote, "by reason of his cover and the smoke, except for the flash of his muskets, and his waving flags. Those red flags are accumulating at the wall every moment, and they maddened us as the same color does the bull. Webb's men are falling fast, and he is among them to direct and encourage; but however well they may now do, with that walled enemy in front, with more than a dozen flags to Webb's three, it soon becomes apparent that in not many minutes they will be overpowered, or that none will be alive for the enemy to overpower."

Union Reinforcements Came Quickly

Haskell rode off to find reinforcements, which were sent to the Angle in a hurry by commanders south of the breach. The immediate availability of these troops helped save the Union line at Gettysburg, as Haskell vividly described: "In the briefest time I saw five friendly colors hurrying to the aid of the imperiled three; each color represented true, battle-tried men, that had not turned back from

Rebel fire that day nor yesterday, though their ranks were saddly thinned. . . .

"From my position on horseback, I could see that the enemy's right . . . was beginning to stagger and to break. 'See,' I said to the men, 'see the "chivalry," see the gray-backs run!' The men saw, and as they swept to their places . . . and opened fire, they roared; and this in a manner that said more plainly than words—for the deaf could have seen it in their faces, and the blind could have heard it in their voices—*the crest is safe.*"

Cannons Fired at Point-Blank Range

At the climax of Pickett's Charge, the attackers faced artillery trained on them at point-blank range. And cannoneers, ordered to keep the big guns firing, had to hold their ground against an enemy shooting at them with rifles. Illustrating just how close the Rebels were to the Union cannons is the command given by Andrew Cowan of the 1st New York Battery, who faced a Confederate breakthrough. The order, inscribed on the battery's monument, was succinct: "Double canister at ten yards!"

The South Feared a Counterattack

As the defeated Confederates retreated in disarray back across the open fields, now covered with dead and wounded comrades, Lee rode out to meet them and offer whatever solace he could. A number of soldiers remembered that Pickett himself was in tears; when asked by his commander to reform his division, he replied, "General Lee, I have no division now."

Of great concern to the Confederate leaders who were still on their feet was the possibility of a Union counterattack, and so their time was spent reorganizing and rallying shattered units and preparing reserves to meet a Federal charge. But an attack never came, and the guns gradually grew silent on both sides of the field.

A British Tourist Observed the Rebel Command

A number of "neutral" foreign observers were on the battlefield during the fighting at Gettysburg, but Arthur Fremantle is likely the most famous. A British army officer, Fremantle traveled extensively throughout the United States before the battle. He met Longstreet on June 27 and spent the next week or so in and around the general's headquarters, traveling freely behind the Confederate lines or watching the action from atop a tall, well-placed tree. He witnessed the morning meeting between Longstreet, Lee, Hood, and Heth on July 2 and later heard the original reports that Hood had been wounded and Barksdale killed.

Fremantle didn't see the climax of the battle, however. On July 3, he rode north to try to get into the Lutheran Seminary's cupola, then in Rebel hands. But constant crossfire thwarted his efforts. He returned to Longstreet's headquarters later that day, hoping to observe Pickett's Charge from there. But he was too late; when he reached Longstreet, the dejected general told him that the attack had been repulsed and the battle was lost.

Farnsworth Led a Doomed Charge

Late in the afternoon of July 3, believing that he could break the far right of the Rebel line, Union cavalry commander Judson Kilpatrick ordered one of the most doomed charges of the battle. He sent Elon Farnsworth and his mounted troops to attack a strong Confederate position over rocky, wooded terrain. Farnsworth was shocked at the order and made his thoughts known to Kilpatrick, but he agreed to follow it nonetheless. One of the Rebels facing the attack later described Farnsworth's charge as the "most gallant" action he had ever seen:

"He led his brigade, riding well ahead of his men, in a charge against my battery and the infantry supporters. We were so filled with admiration of his bravery that we were reluctant to kill him and so called out to him to surrender, as his position was hopeless.

He replied by emptying his revolver and then hurling it at us and drawing his saber, when we shot him through the body, killing him. His men were nearly all killed, wounded, or captured, very few escaping to their own lines."

Aftermath

Helping the Wounded Was Sometimes Impossible

When day broke on July 4 and Union parties were sent out to help the Confederate wounded writhing on the field, some found themselves being fired upon by a picket line set up to mask the Army of Northern Virginia's withdrawal. Only the soldiers clearly associated with ambulances were let alone. Consequently, in some cases, it was the men of their own regiments who were responsible for prolonging the agony of the wounded Southerners caught in no-man's-land.

Despite the risk, or perhaps unaware of it, Union colonel Charles Wainwright decided to make a tour of the battlefield to impress the details on his mind. He rode out between the lines on horseback and soon encountered the weak calls of the Confederate wounded pleading to be moved. Returning to his lines, he appealed to some regimental surgeons to do something for the men, but they refused because the wounded did not belong to their unit.

"I fear that I should be very hard on such fellows if I had the power," Wainwright said in disgust. "As a rule, the wounded of both sides are treated alike by our surgeons."

Some members of the 14th Connecticut couldn't stand the sight of unattended Confederates "laying out there in hundreds, moaning or shrieking in pain—as indeed we had heard them all through the night previous." Taking a chance on getting shot themselves, they went out and brought in as many wounded as they could.

It Was Mercy "To Die Instantly"

Union soldier Van Willard, a Wisconsin volunteer, wrote an eloquent account of his experiences at Gettysburg, including a description of the field after the fighting on Culp's Hill: "On the crest of that ridge there is an open field of perhaps two acres. On that little space there could not have been less than five hundred dead and wounded. One could not look in any direction, let him turn which ever way he would, without seeing scores of dead and wounded men, shot in every way a bullet could hit them, lying just as they had fallen. Some of them had been killed instantly, others had struggled fiercely with death, tearing the earth with their hands, dying at last with expressions of the most horrible agony lingering on their distorted features. Some had died as if without a struggle, others had been thrown into the most terrible convulsions, their bodies crumpled and twisted in every shape, their limbs extended or thrown out from the body, their mouths open and eyes glaring with the ghastly light of death.

"One who has never been on a battle field . . . can form but a poor idea of its horrors. It is mercy to him, if he is to fall, to die instantly, for the suffering of the badly wounded is beyond description."

Lee Retreated in the Rain

Around noon on July 4 it started to rain. By late afternoon, the downpour became torrential, turning dirt roads into mud holes and running streams. Herculean efforts by the Confederates were required to get their wagon trains of wounded soldiers onto the road and headed toward Chambersburg. Hour after hour, until far into the night, the train grew longer and longer until at last the final wagon was rolling.

Lee gradually became satisfied that Meade did not intend to attack, so when the wounded were all on the road, he ordered his army to begin its retreat. It was still raining, and immediate pursuit was unlikely because of the darkness and weather. By the morning of July 5, the last of the Confederates, save for the dead and seriously wounded, had left Gettysburg. The Union army found itself alone on the field.

Lincoln Was Frustrated with Meade

Meade sent cavalry troops to harass the retreating army, but he didn't follow up his victory with a major attack. Had he done so, when the Confederates were cut apart and stretched so thin, many historians believe he would have won the war.

The White House and War Department were angered by his cautious conduct, and the president himself sat down to compose a letter to Meade. "My dear general," it read, in part, "I do not believe you appreciate the magnitude of the misfortune involved in Lee's escape. He was within your easy grasp, and to have closed in on him would, in connection with our other late successes, have ended the war. As it is, the war will be prolonged indefinitely. . . . Your golden opportunity is gone, and I am distressed immeasurably because of it."

Lincoln never sent the letter, perhaps thinking it would be ungracious to do so. But in March 1864 he gave Ulysses S. Grant control of all Federal armies, effectively depriving Meade of his command.

Longstreet Was Blamed

Rightly or wrongly, Longstreet was widely blamed for the Confederate defeat at Gettysburg, and he spent the remainder of his life defending his actions there. A native of South Carolina, Longstreet was a West Point graduate, although he was much better in athletics than in academics. At West Point, he met Ulysses Grant, who became a lifelong friend; he also met Grant's cousin Louise, whom he soon married. Like many Civil War generals, he was a veteran of the Mexican War. At Chapultepec, he fought alongside George Pickett and was seriously wounded in the leg.

When the Civil War broke out, Longstreet resigned from the U.S. Army and joined the Rebel cause. After three of his children died of scarlet fever, in January 1862, his devotion to the military grew deeper. He worked closely with Robert E. Lee, who called him his "Old War Horse," although they disagreed on tactics more than a few times. At Antietam, he performed admirably, but the defeat at Gettysburg became his legacy—one he would never live down.

The Town Was Battered and Scarred

Three days of combat had left the Gettysburg area in a terrible state. During the battle, the 170,000 combatants had fired 569 tons of metal, resulting in about 50,000 casualties—10,000 killed, 30,000 wounded, 10,000 missing or captured. The wounded exceeded the entire population of surrounding Adams County. As well, some 3,000 horses and mules had died. Dead men and horses littered the field, some places in piles. While the troops left behind struggled to bury the 7,000 battlefield dead (3,000 more died later of wounds), it was an enormous job, and some corpses were not buried for more than a month. The sight of bodies swelling in the summer heat was sickening, and the stench made walking the fields difficult. Hordes of flies added to the miserable conditions; the potential for an outbreak of disease was serious.

For years afterward it was obvious to anyone that a major battle had been fought at Gettysburg. Few houses and barns escaped damage. Fences were torn down, and trees, or what was left of them, were testimony to the ferocity of the fighting. Crops were destroyed, and many people sued the government for compensation, although none of the litigants was ever paid.

A Property Owner Received Little Compensation

Abraham Brian was a free black man who owned a small farm and orchard just south of town, near Zeigler's Grove. He left when he heard that Confederates were approaching, and his buildings and land were taken over by the Federals—Alexander Hays used the Brian house as his headquarters. On July 3, the farm was the scene of heavy fighting, as elements of the far left of the Rebel line broke through Union positions under withering fire before being driven back. Photos taken soon after the battle show that the Brian house and barn were heavily damaged, and when the owner petitioned for restitution, he was awarded only fifteen dollars. He was forced to sell and went to work at a nearby hotel. Today the rebuilt Brian house and barn are at the center of a part of the battlefield undergoing extensive restoration.

The Dead Were Buried Differently

The soldiers from the two armies were buried differently. The Union dead tended to be buried individually. If their identities were known, a crude headstone was set up. The Confederate dead were thrown into long, shallow trenches. No body was buried very deeply, so it was not uncommon to see a hand or head sticking out of the soil, especially after a heavy rain. The horses were often burned, their bones later used as fertilizer.

A Famous Map of Graves Is Likely Incorrect

Reports of mass burials of dead Confederates on the grounds of the Rose farm, between the Peach Orchard and Devil's Den, are likely exaggerated (although there is little doubt that a significant number of slain soldiers were buried there). The erroneous information likely came from a map drawn by a civil engineer named Elliott who visited the battlefield in the fall of 1863, before many troops were disinterred for reburial at the new Soldier's National Cemetery. His well-known map indicates two trenches within the boundaries of the 230-acre Rose farm, one labeled "500 Rebel Graves," the other "400 Rebel Graves." Calculations from casualty lists of the units that fought in and around the farm show that these numbers are highly unlikely, however. Historians speculate that Elliott got wrong information, which he then included on his map, or that he himself wrote down incorrect data, intentionally or unintentionally.

The Rose farmhouse still stands. The barn burned down in the early 1900s, and only its foundation is visible today.

Only One Civilian Was Killed

The only civilian killed during the three days of fighting was twenty-year-old Virginia Mary Wade, who was struck by a stray bullet on July 3 as she was baking bread for Union soldiers in the kitchen of her sister's home on Baltimore Street, near Cemetery Hill. During the battle, the house was hit repeatedly by musket fire as Confederates attacked the heights and Union soldiers responded; at least one round of cannon fire struck the house, too.

It is thought that Wade died instantly, although her body, kept in the basement, wasn't buried for days after the battle. The two-story house still stands and is a popular tourist attraction, especially the basement, which some say is haunted by her ghost. Wade is buried at nearby Evergreen Cemetery; her grave is marked by a well-visited monument.

She was engaged to a Union soldier, Johnston Skelley, who, unknown to Wade, was captured during the Battle of Winchester and held prisoner in Virginia during the Gettysburg Campaign. He died there on July 12, a little more than a week after his bride-to-be was killed.

The Trostle Farm Bore Marks of Carnage

The farm owned by Peter Trostle just north of the Peach Orchard was occupied by Peter's son and daughter-in-law, Catherine, at the time of the battle. They were forced out when the fighting began. On July 2, Sickles used the place as his headquarters after moving his troops to positions nearby. The occupation and heavy fighting on the farm did much damage—a hole from a cannonball is still visible near the roofline of the barn. Sickles was wounded on the grounds, as well.

After the war, Catherine petitioned for restitution for damages, which included the destruction of "32 acres of grass, 27 acres of wheat, 9 acres of corn" and "20 tons of hay." Her petition also notes that "16 dead horses were left close by the door and probably 100 on the farm" (a photo of the house taken on July 6 backs up her claim; it shows a pile of dead horses amid the wreckage). The most vivid part of her claim, however, notes the "her husband, Abraham Trostle, has become insane, and is now in the Lunatic Asylum."

Private Culp Died on His Family's Hill

Before the battle, Culp's Hill was owned by Henry Culp, whose nephew Wesley romped through its woods as a child. When Wesley was older, he moved to Virginia to follow his employer. When the Civil War started, Wesley joined the Confederate army, becoming part of Jackson's famous "Stonewall Brigade." His unit was sent to Gettysburg, and when Confederates advanced through the streets on July 1, Wesley stopped to visit family members still living in town. On July 2, Wesley found himself fighting on Culp's Hill. He was killed there the next day, within sight of his family home, on the same heights he had explored years before.

Details Didn't Reach Richmond for Two Weeks

By July 4, telegraphic communications between Richmond and Lee's army had been cut, and the flooded Potomac River made it difficult for couriers and reporters to get back to Virginia with news. For the next two weeks, the Confederate capital was filled with rumors and unconfirmed reports about what had happened in Pennsylvania.

Many thought Lee had won. A Richmond newspaper reported on July 7 that the Confederates had triumphed at Gettysburg, that the Union army was retreating toward Baltimore, and "General Lee is pursuing."

In a diary entry for July 7, the head of the Confederate Bureau of War noted that "General Lee has delivered a great battle at Gettysburg, Pennsylvania, with Meade's army. It began on Thursday, July 2nd. We have only Yankee accounts, but these inspire hope of a victory. . . . A telegram from the operator at Martinsburg states that on the 6th General Lee had captured 40,000 of the enemy; that Hill in the center fell back as if borne by the enemy who fell into the trap, while Longstreet and Ewell closed in on the flanks and made this capture."

As varied reports swirled around the capital, the general attitude seemed to change from day to day. In his July 8 diary entry, war department clerk J. B. Jones wrote that "the hills around Gettysburg are said to be covered with the dead and wounded of the Yankee Army of the Potomac. . . . The New York and Pennsylvania papers are reported to have declared for Peace." He later noted, however, that "the absence of dispatches from General Lee himself is beginning to cause distrust."

It wasn't until July 17, two weeks after the fighting at Gettysburg, that accurate accounts of the battle reached Richmond and were published in the papers. On that day, Jones wrote, "the armies of the Confederate States are recoiling at all points, and a settled gloom is apparent on many weak faces."

Lincoln Noted Fourth of July Events

During an impromptu speech on July 7, Lincoln noted all the historic events that occurred on the Fourth of July, including the signing of the Declaration of Independence; the deaths of John Adams, Thomas Jefferson, and James Monroe; and the Confederate defeat at Vicksburg and retreat from the north:

"On this last Fourth of July just passed, when we have a gigantic rebellion, at the bottom of which is an effort to overthrow the principle that all men are created equal, we have the surrender of a most powerful position and army on that very day. And not only so, but in a succession of battles in Pennsylvania, near to us, through three days, so rapidly fought that they might be called one great battle, on the first, second, and third of the month of July; and on the fourth the cohorts of those who opposed the Declaration that all men are created equal turned tail and ran."

Lee Suggested a Move on Washington

On July 8, Lee wrote a letter to Confederate president Jefferson Davis that outlined some recommended military maneuvers and described his mood. "From information gathered from the papers I believe that the troops from North Carolina and the coast of Virginia, under Generals Foster and Dix, have been ordered to the Potomac and that recently additional reinforcements have been sent from the coast of South Carolina to General Banks.

"If I am correct in my opinion this will liberate most of the troops in those regions and should not your Excellency have already done so I earnestly recommend that all that can be spared be concentrated on the Upper Rappahannock under General Beauregard with directions to cross that river and make a demonstration on Washington. This course will answer the double purpose of affording protection to the capital at Richmond and relieving the pressure upon this army. . . .

"I hope your Excellency will understand that I am not in the least discouraged or that my faith in the protection of an All Merciful Providence, or in the fortitude of this army is at all shaken. But though conscious that the enemy has been much shattered in the recent battle, I am aware that he can be easily reinforced, while no addition can be made to our numbers."

Hospital Conditions Were Gruesome

Homes, inns, barns, and tents became temporary hospitals for the wounded of Gettysburg. For lack of a better place, treatment of wounds—often quick surgery—was sometimes done outdoors. One woman who came to town to assist the surgeons remembered that a long platform set up in the woods was used as an operating table "and for seven days it literally ran blood. A wagon stood near rapidly filling with amputated legs and arms. When wholly filled, this gruesome spectacle withdrew from sight and returned as soon as possible for another load. So appalling was the number of wounded as yet unsuccored, so helpless seemed the few who were battling against tremendous odds to save life, and so overwhelming was the demand for any kind of aid that could be given quickly that one's senses were benumbed."

Another observer despaired at the horrific atmosphere: "The condition of things here beggars all description. Our dead lie unburied, and our wounded neglected. Our wounded in numbers have been drowned by the sudden rising of the waters around, and thousands of them are still naked and starving. God pity us!"

A Hospital Camp Treated North and South Alike

After three long weeks of miserable treatment for the wounded, authorities opened a centralized hospital camp in an attempt to improve conditions. Located about a mile east of town, Camp Letterman included four hundred tents, each with a dozen beds. Some eight thousand soldiers were eventually transferred to the facility. As they were admitted, officers were separated from enlisted men, but Union and Confederate wounded were otherwise closely integrated. This held true right up to the point of burial at the hospital cemetery, conveniently set up just beyond the tents, next to an embalming station and a "dead house," where the deceased were processed. The gravesites were perfectly spaced and legibly identified—a soldier from New York resting next to one from Virginia, a corporal from

Alabama laying beside a sergeant from Indiana. The mortality rate at the camp was high, but this was to be expected, since most of the patients were the most severely wounded.

On September 23, camp officials arranged a banquet for the patients still recuperating. Confederate and Union soldiers attended the event together. The tables were set with platters of chicken, ham, oysters, pies, and ice cream—items most of the men hadn't seen or tasted in years. Camp Letterman stayed in operation for almost four months. It closed in November, the same week the new national cemetery was dedicated.

An "Angel" Helped Bury the Dead

Before the war, Elizabeth Thorn assisted her husband in his duties as caretaker of Gettysburg's Evergreen Cemetery, located at the top of Cemetery Hill. The couple lived in the distinctive cemetery gatehouse along with their three young sons and her parents. When Peter Thorn enlisted in the Union Army, however, Elizabeth was left to care for the cemetery and handle local burials on her own. When the fighting at Gettysburg began, Elizabeth and her family left the gatehouse—after she prepared a meal for a handful of Union generals. She returned as soon as the battle was over, and the cemetery's president asked her to begin burying the hundreds of slain soldiers who were being brought to the gatehouse grounds. By all accounts, she worked diligently at this trying task for many long days, even though she was six months' pregnant at the time. Today, a sculpture in the cemetery honors the work done by Thorn, now known as the "Angel of Gettysburg."

A Second Invasion Soon Arrived

Within weeks of the battle, as soon as the trains started running again, Gettysburg faced another invasion: visitors from near and far descended on the town. They had a variety of motives. There were those who came to help and those coming to search—wives, mothers, and fathers not knowing for certain if their loved one was still alive or where he might be among the scores of hospitals on the vast field. There were those who came to profit, including morticians offering assistance in exhuming bodies and embalming them for shipment back home. There were relic hunters, seeking bullets, bayonets, and other items that could be hawked on the street as mementos of the great battle. There were newspaper correspondents with numerous publications to satisfy.

Most bothersome, perhaps, to the residents were the curious. They came in legions in their Sunday finery just to gawk and stare, gasp and exclaim at the ghastly sights of an actual battlefield, but they had no inclination to assist in any way.

Looting Was a Problem

Looting and souvenir collecting were rampant on the battlefield, and the government wanted to reclaim as much useful military matériel as it possibly could. On July 7, Union captain William Smith was sent from Washington to Gettysburg "to collect all property left by both armies in the vicinity." It was a tremendous task. On his first day in town, Smith saw seventy-six wagons leaving the battle area; he stopped and searched thirty of them—every one contained government property.

Smith and a newly formed cavalry unit launched a systematic search for stolen materials. The canvass produced bountiful results, with weapons and blankets being uncovered by the wagonload over a fifteen-mile radius. One farmer had a cache that included ten muskets, a saber, two cartridge boxes, fifteen blankets, fifteen tent sections, twenty-five knapsacks, some clothing, and a horse. A six-pound cannon was found lowered into a well. In many cases, the looters were ordered to load the matériel into their wagons themselves and join the searchers' convoy. Those who refused were dealt with harshly. "I am not very careful," Smith wrote, "how I treat such parties."

A New National Cemetery Was Created

A week after the battle, Pennsylvania governor Andrew Curtin visited the field. He was appalled by the devastation, and by the treatment of the dead. He quickly devised a plan whereby the state would defray the cost of removing any Pennsylvanian killed in the fighting and sending the remains back to his hometown. He also agreed to establish a national cemetery at Gettysburg, one of the first of its kind in the country. The site would be on seventeen acres purchased for $2,475.87 atop Cemetery Hill. Under the plan, Pennsylvania would provide a burial spot for any soldier killed in the battle; the soldier's home state would then be assessed for the body's removal and preparation of the grounds.

The date of the ceremony to dedicate the cemetery was moved from October 23 to November 16 to accommodate the event's main speaker, renowned orator Edward Everett. Organizers were surprised when Abraham Lincoln accepted the courtesy invitation extended to him. Two weeks before the event, the president was offered time after Everett's speech to make "a few appropriate remarks." The brief address he gave became one of history's greatest speeches.

Landmarks Were Named After the Battle

The names of some of the battlefield's most famous landmarks weren't in wide use until after the battle was over. At the time of the fighting, "Round Top" referred to only the larger of the area's two peaks, what is now called Big Round Top. Before 1863, today's Little Round Top was known by a variety of names, including "Sugar Loaf," "Broad Top," and "Rock Hill." Likewise, even though local farmer Henry Culp did own the land that included the high ground southeast of town in 1863, this feature wasn't generally known as Culp's Hill until after the battle occurred.

"Devil's Den" was a well-known local landmark before the battle, however. The jumble of giant granite boulders formed by volcanic activity 180 million years ago was something of a local tourist destination and picnic spot before 1863—even though it was rumored to be both the home of enormous black snakes as well as the site of a large Native American battle (arrowheads reportedly were found in abundance there, but the legend of its being the place of significant pre-Civil War fighting is as yet unfounded).

Invading Rebels Sensed the North's Manpower Advantage

In the years after the battle, one resident recalled touring the field with an ex-Confederate officer, who described the thoughts of some rebels when Lee's troops entered Pennsylvania. "Coming down all along the route in the Cumberland Valley and seeing the bountiful crops, and coming down through the towns of Shippensburg, Chambersburg, and Carlisle, and seeing the many able-bodied young men standing on the streets looking at them and seeing the many able-bodied young men coming out of the shops at quitting time, they were disheartened. One officer said to his fellow officer, what was the use of us coming over here to fight those people—why they could raise another army again as large as they have now and feed them too."

An Important Landmark Was Destroyed

During the battle, the western face of Cemetery Hill was covered by a thick group of trees known as Zeigler's Grove. The importance of this landmark has been underappreciated in many accepted histories of the fighting; some researchers believe the grove might have been a key component of Lee's July 3 plan of attack. After the battle, a number of Confederate dead were found in these woods, suggesting that the assault here was fierce, as it was farther south at the Angle.

Unfortunately for historians, Zeigler's Grove was felled for lumber in the years after the battle. Many veterans who returned to the field late in life saw a greatly altered landscape. Today, the place where the grove had been lies between the former sites of the park visitors center and the Cyclorama, where parking lots and other construction mask the area's historical importance. Further complicating research is the modern development that completely obscures the view Lee had of Zeigler's Grove from his headquarters on Seminary Ridge.

The Trolley Downplayed Cemetery Hill

The building of a trolley system on the battlefield in the late 1880s downplayed Cemetery Hill's significance in the battle's history. By the 1890s, visitors arriving in Gettysburg by train could transfer downtown onto a trolley designed to take them in the direction of the Round Tops. With the trolley in place, the southern portions of the battlefield became more accessible, more publicized, and therefore more important. East Cemetery Hill was the last stop on the trolley route, and Culp's Hill was excluded altogether. Even today, far fewer visitors tour Culp's Hill and the battleground along Cemetery Hill's north slope than they do Cemetery Ridge, Little Round Top, and Devil's Den.

Officials Work to Restore the Park's Appearance

In recent years, officials at the Gettysburg National Military Park have worked to restore the landscape to its 1863 appearance. The most dramatic of these efforts was the demolition of the Gettysburg National Tower in July 2001. The four-hundred-foot tower, built in 1974 on historically important land along the Taneytown Road, offered sweeping views of the town and battlefield, but it was visible from just about every part of the park, and many considered it an eyesore.

Other restoration efforts involve cutting back or eliminating woodlands that have grown thick in the past hundred years, particularly along Plum Run, which cuts across the fields below Cemetery Ridge and Little Round Top. As well, trees in Sherfy's Peach Orchard are being replanted after disease killed many that had been growing there.

Equestrian Monuments Tell a Story

Today, a number of equestrian monuments pay tribute to the generals who commanded troops during the battle. At Gettysburg, these monuments follow the traditional symbolic code that indicates the honored general's fate. If all four of the horse's hooves are on the ground, the rider was unharmed during the battle. If one of the hooves is raised, the rider was wounded in the fighting. If two hooves are raised, the rider was killed.

Only one equestrian monument at Gettysburg does not follow tradition. The bronze horse carrying the figure of James Longstreet—dedicated in 1998 and located near Pitzer Woods on the right side of Seminary Ridge—has one hoof in the air even though the general was not wounded at Gettysburg.

The Largest Monument Is Pennsylvania's

The Pennsylvania Memorial is the largest monument on the battlefield today. It stands prominently on the center of Cemetery Ridge. Built in 1910 at a cost of $182,000, the monument is topped with a twenty-one-foot-high Goddess of Victory and Peace, made of bronze from cannon barrels used in the war. Each side of the monument honors a branch of service, and its eight statues represent important state sons who were at Gettysburg. The base features the names of 34,500 Pennsylvania soldiers who took part in the battle.

About a mile to the west, along Seminary Ridge, is the Virginia Memorial, which honors both Robert E. Lee and the Virginians who served under him. It is thought that Lee watched Pickett's Charge from where the monument stands today, but some historians believe the general was actually farther north, near where the North Carolina Memorial now stands.

The War Took an Enormous Toll

Experts estimate that 2.5 percent of the entire population of the United States was killed in the Civil War, and while that percentage might not seem huge—if a war today killed the same percentage of the country's population, it would equal some seven million deaths.

The average age of a Civil War soldier was just under twenty-six. More than 40 percent of the Civil War dead were never identified. And while the fighting of Civil War battles was deadly, disease was even more so: two out of every three deaths during the war were caused by disease instead of battle.

Information in this book was excerpted from *They Met at Gettysburg*, third edition, by Edward J. Stackpole (1982); *The Battle of Gettysburg: A Guided Tour*, revised and updated edition, by Edward J. Stackpole and Wilbur S. Nye (1998); *Witness to Gettysburg*, by Richard Wheeler (2006); *Gettysburg: The Story of the Battle with Maps* (2013); *Pickett's Charge*, edited by Richard Rollins (2004); *The Civil War Soldier: A Photographic Journey*, by Ray A. Carson (2000); *Debris of Battle: The Wounded of Gettysburg*, by Gerald A. Patterson (1997); *North with Lee and Jackson*, by James A. Kegel (1996); *Lee's Real Plan at Gettysburg*, by Troy D. Harman (2003); *Damn Dutch: Pennsylvania Germans at Gettysburg*, by David Valuska and Christian B. Keller (2004); *The New Annals of the Civil War*, edited by Peter Cozzens and Robert I. Girardi (2004); *With the 3rd Wisconsin Badgers*, edited by Steven S. Rabb (1999); and *Reliving the Civil War: A Reenactor's Handbook*, by R. Lee Hadden (1996); all published by Stackpole Books.

Additional information was provided by the National Park Service (www.nps.gov/gett).

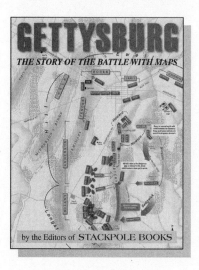